Polka Dot Girls

Designed. Original. Treasured.

By
Kristie Kerr & Paula Yarnes

ISBN: 978-0-9840-312-0-308

Printed in the United States of America

1st Printing

Contents

Dedication

Dedicated to the girls who inspire us:

Anja who does funny accents...

JoJo who defies all odds...

Catelyn who is a SURVIVOR...

Lucy who LOVES unconditionally...

Betty who LIGHTS UP THE ROOM...

Dottie who loves tutus AND fishing poles...

Meg who is so funny she could possibly be the next Lucille Ball...

Ling who is NOT AFRAID to speak her mind...

Natalie who can organize like nobody's business...

Jeorgia who has AMAZING COURAGE...

and **Lily** who is simply sweet!

You amaze us.

Go change the world.

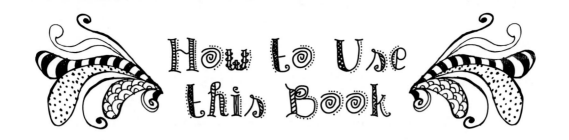

It seems easy enough, right? Like you really shouldn't need a page just to tell you how to use this book. And yet, here we are. We are nothing if we're not efficient!

Ok. This resource was written as a tool for use in a large group, small group or even for your family to use. Obviously, your specific needs may vary according to the size and make up of your group, but we have hopefully provided you with enough options that you have plenty of... well, options.

Each chapter starts with a large group lesson. This is something that can be taught by one teacher or even a variety of leaders. These lessons are designed to appeal to all age groups – so bring all your girls together for this part of the session. There are stories and illustrations provided, but feel free to add in your own thoughts, insights and stories! The girls will love to hear about your own personal experiences and perspective.

Following the large group time, there are questions for small group discussion. These are broken down by grade level (K-1, 2-3, and 4-5) – so this would be a great time to divide the girls into smaller groups with separate leaders so that the discussion can be

tailored to fit their level of experience and understanding. (If you don't have enough leaders to do small groups, keep the girls together and alternate questions from the various age level discussion questions.) Close out your small group time with a time of prayer. Invite the girls to pray for each other and take turns praying out loud. Not only will you learn a lot about your girls during this time, their little hearts will be bonded together when they spend time praying for one another.

Then it's craft time! We've included lots of fun ideas for you to do as a group. Make sure you do adequate preparation depending on the age and skill level of your girls. Nothing is more frustrating than running out of time because you spent too much time cutting things out or waiting for glue to dry. (By the way... glue dries REALLY slow. Even slower when you want it to dry fast. Just our experience anyway....)

Lastly, we've included some pages to be photocopied and sent home. They include a weekly challenge for the girls, age appropriate activity sheets, and a parent partner. These are intended to give the girls some fun tools to work on throughout the week and to let the parents keep up with what their daughters are learning.

And the MOST important thing to remember is to MAKE IT WORK FOR YOU. Every group is unique and different, so feel free to add, subtract, edit, rewrite, and rework anything you find here. Find out what works and stick with it and don't be afraid to chuck the stuff that isn't working.

Our job is simple — but it couldn't be more important. We get the amazing privilege of teaching these sweet girls about Jesus. We pray the material gives you practical tools to do just that. But above and beyond all that, remember that your gift of time and interest in these girls' lives will impact them far greater than any lesson or illustration. You are literally demonstrating for them what it means to be a woman who loves Jesus. Be patient. Be loving. Be fun. Be there.

We wish you all the best as you teach your girls what it means to be a Polka Dot Girl!

Relationships

We Need Each Other

WHAT'S THE POINT?

GOD CREATED US TO SHARE OUR LIVES WITH OTHER PEOPLE.

theme verse

Treat people in the same way that you want them to treat you.

Luke 6:31 (CEB)

related bible story

God gives Adam a companion

Genesis 2

❀ Large Group Lesson ❀

It's not very much fun being by yourself. Can you imagine what it would be like if you didn't have any friends or family? I don't think that would be very much fun at all!

God made us with a desire for relationships. There is something inside of us that needs to have other people in our lives.

The Bible tells us that God created everything – the entire universe and everything in it was created by Him! But that wasn't His greatest creation. Oh no… the greatest thing God made was US! The Bible tells us that the first person God created was a man named Adam. He was the very first person on the earth.

3

Genesis 2:7 says, "*Then the Lord God formed the man from the dust of the ground. He breathed the breath of life into the man's nostrils, and the man became a living person.*"

Adam lived in the beautiful Garden of Eden. It had everything he could have ever wanted inside of it. But one thing was missing: Someone with whom Adam could share his life. In Genesis 2:18, God said, "*It is not good for the man to be alone.*" God knew that we needed other people in our lives to talk to, encourage and support, and to be there for one another.

So God made beautiful Eve, the very first woman. (Girls Rock!!) Not only was she Adam's wife – she was Adam's friend. The Bible calls her Adam's helper or companion. A companion is someone who is by your side as you go on a journey. God gave Adam a companion to walk with him through life. No matter what was going to happen in Adam's life, he now had someone who would be alongside him!

Isn't that cool! Out of all the cool things that God gives us (and He gives us LOTS of really cool things) friendship and companionship are one of His best ideas! God doesn't make us go through life all by ourselves. He gives us family and friends, pastors and teachers, neighbors and classmates to share our lives with us.

I am so thankful for all the relationships that God has given to me. I am thankful for my Mom and Dad who have loved me and taken good care of me. I am thankful for the friends that God has given me who make me laugh and listen to me cry. I am thankful for teachers who have taught me how to do things and helped me learn all kinds of important stuff. (Yes… even the MATH teachers… even though I REALLY hated math class!!!)

God doesn't want us to go through life by ourselves. He KNOWS that it is not good for us to be alone, so He gives us people to share our lives. I know that sometimes it can feel like you are all alone, but the truth is that God has provided LOTS of people who care about you, love you, and want to be your companion as you grow and learn about life.

POLKA DOT POINTERS

Take a minute and think of 3 people that are COMPANIONS in your life. Maybe it's your Mom and Dad? Maybe a special friend? Maybe your teacher or pastor? God has blessed you with lots of people who care about you!!

God blesses us by giving us people in our lives. They are a gift to us. And just like any gift we are given, we need to appreciate it and take care of it. We need to be thankful for the friends and family God has given us and make sure we work really hard at being a good friend, daughter, student, classmate, and family member.

But let's be really honest. Our relationships are one of our greatest blessings, but they can also be one of our biggest problems! We can have fights with our friends. Our brothers can pick on us. We can get frustrated with our parents. Our teachers can make us mad and our neighbors can hurt our feelings.

God knows how important your relationships are to you, and so He wants to help you with them! The Bible is full of instructions to help us work out all the problems in our relationships. There are things that God tells us to do to be a good friend. He shows us what kind of attitude we should have toward our parents. He helps us by showing us how to treat people who aren't kind and loving to us. God wants to help you with your relationships!

No matter what kind of questions you have about your relationships, God has the answers. He promises to help you with ALL the relationships in your lives because He knows how important they are.

In the next few weeks and months, we are going to take a look at all the relationships in our lives. We are going to check out what the Bible has to say about being a good friend. We are going to learn how to treat the people around us and how to behave in order to take really, really good care of all the relationships God has given to us.

God gives us really specific ideas as to how we can take care of our relationships, but there is one scripture in the Bible that will be our theme throughout the next few weeks. It is a magic secret weapon that you can use in ANY relationship, at ANY time, ANY place – no matter what the situation may be. Are you ready? Do you want to hear God's magic super secret weapon for having good relationships?

Ok....... Here it is......... are you SURE you're ready? Cause it s a REALLY big deal. Ok......... I think you're ready now.

Treat people in the same way that you want them to treat you.
– Luke 6:31 (CEB)

It seems pretty simple, right? Treat other people the way YOU want to be treated. Any time you are faced with a situation and you wonder what you should say or do, all you have to do is ask yourself the question, "How would I want someone to treat ME if I was in the same situation?" and you'll have your answer.

We should treat people the way we want to be treated. If you are wondering if you should say something, ask yourself how you would feel if someone said that exact same thing about YOU. If you are wondering if you should do something, ask yourself how you would feel if someone did the same thing to you.

God wants you to treat other people the way you want to be treated. When you do this, your relationships will grow stronger. And strong relationships are super important because they are such a valuable part of our life.

Here are 3 reasons why your relationships are so important!

⇒ 1. Your relationships help you grow.

Sheila never really felt like she was good at anything. While her friends were getting better at tennis and playing the piano, Sheila simply watched from the sidelines. She really wanted to be good at something, but she just couldn't seem to find the thing that made her heart sing.

But when she started third grade, she had a new teacher named Mrs. Schneider. Mrs. Schneider seemed to see something in Sheila that she had never seen in herself. She noticed that Sheila really enjoyed the times in class where they got to work on computers. So one day, she asked Sheila to create a special presentation for the class.

Sheila found herself super nervous about the project, but super excited too! The more she worked on the project, the more she realized how much she really enjoyed creating things on the computer. It came really easy to her, and she found herself working for hours without even noticing!

When Sheila grew up, she got a job working with computers! She loves her work and is really, really good at it. There are many times when she thinks about Mrs. Schneider who helped her discover her love of computers. She often wonders if she would be doing what she is doing without the encouragement and support that Mrs. Schneider gave her in the third grade.

God will bring people into your life that will help you grow! He will use them to show you new things, inspire you to try something different, and even help you find your gifts and talents. You will have friends who will cheer you on as you discover the things you are good at. You have family members who will help you see something in yourself that you may have never seen on your own. God uses other people to help us grow in all kinds of areas of our lives!

The second reason relationships are so important is:

⇨ 2. Your relationships help you rub off the rough edges.

Katie had developed a bad habit. When other people were trying to tell her a story, she would interrupt them. She wasn't trying to be rude, she would just think of what she wanted to say and blurt it out without thinking.

One day, her very best friend in the whole wide world, Nicki, was telling her something when she once again jumped in and interrupted. Nicki took a deep breath and gently stopped her and said, "Katie, I was telling you a story and you stopped and interrupted me. You are my best friend, but it really hurts my feelings when you do that."

At first, Katie was mad! "I don't do that!" she thought to herself! But then she realized that Nicki was right… she really hadn't been listening and had rudely interrupted her friend. She had a decision to make right then. She could get upset at Nicki and storm off, or she could admit that she had gotten into a bad habit and listen to her friend.

"I'm sorry," Katie said. "I shouldn't have interrupted you. Please finish your story."

We ALL have things we need to work on in our lives. NONE of us are perfect, and there are always areas of our lives where we can get rid of some stuff that isn't the best.

And MANY times, God will use the other people in our lives to help us see things that we need to work on. And even though it can be hard to take sometimes, knowing that our friends love us and want to help us makes all the difference. Proverbs 27:6 tells us, "*Wounds from a sincere friend are better than many kisses from an enemy.*" What that means is, even though it's never fun to hear things that we are doing wrong, we can trust that our friends want to help us. We can trust that when they tell us something, they are doing it out of love because they want the best for us.

A good friend will help you stop a bad habit. Your Mom and Dad can help you get over a behavior that isn't good so that you don't hurt other people by your actions. A teacher can show you how to overcome a problem and figure out a new way to do things.

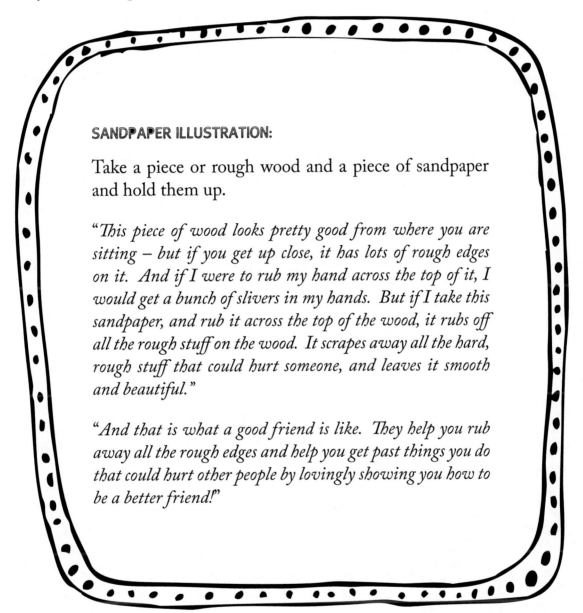

SANDPAPER ILLUSTRATION:

Take a piece or rough wood and a piece of sandpaper and hold them up.

"This piece of wood looks pretty good from where you are sitting – but if you get up close, it has lots of rough edges on it. And if I were to rub my hand across the top of it, I would get a bunch of slivers in my hands. But if I take this sandpaper, and rub it across the top of the wood, it rubs off all the rough stuff on the wood. It scrapes away all the hard, rough stuff that could hurt someone, and leaves it smooth and beautiful."

"And that is what a good friend is like. They help you rub away all the rough edges and help you get past things you do that could hurt other people by lovingly showing you how to be a better friend!"

As iron sharpens iron, so a friend sharpens a friend.
Proverbs 27:17

So, your relationships help you grow, your relationships help rub off the rough edges of your life, and lastly:

➡ **3. Your relationships help you through hard stuff.**

Kara was going through a tough time with her family. Her parents were fighting a lot and her brother and sister were really busy with all of their friends and activities. Kara felt so lonely and sad, and she wasn't sure what to do.

One day her friend Kelsey noticed that something was wrong. She asked Kara if she was ok, and suddenly everything that had been weighing on Kara's heart came rushing out. She told Kara all the things she was feeling and how worried she was about everything. As she shared what was going on in her life, suddenly the weight that had been on her didn't seem quite so heavy anymore.

The people in your life can help get you through the hard things that we all face. Your parents can help you work through a tough season with your friends. Your teachers can help you overcome some fears you might have at school. Your friends can stand beside you when you are facing all kinds of things and remind you that you are not alone. Proverbs 17:17 says, "*A friend is always loyal, and a brother is born to help in time of need.*"

God doesn't want us to go through life alone. He gave us other people to walk through our lives together. It is one of His best gifts and we want to make sure we take really, really good care of it.

Closing Prayer: *Dear God, Thank you for the amazing gift of relationships. Thank you that you have blessed me with friends and family who will walk through my life with me. Help me to treat people the way I want to be treated, and take good care of all the relationships in my life. I love you. Amen.*

Polka Dot Talk

Kindergarten and 1st Grade Group Discussion Questions

1. God said, "It's not good for man to be alone." So he made a companion for Adam. What is a companion?

   a. A companion is a friend.

   b. It is someone who goes on a journey with you.

   c. It is someone who you share your life with.

2. God brings all kinds of special people into our lives. Tell the group about someone who is very special to you. Why is that person important to you?

3. Practice saying the theme verse together a few times. "*Treat people in the same way that you want them to treat you.*" – Luke 6:31 (CEB)

4. God gives us relationships to help us grow. Is there someone in your life who has taught you something or helped you realize something you are good at? Share it with the group!

5. Our relationships can also help "rub off the rough edges" in our lives. What does that mean?

   a. A friend can help you see something that you need to change.

   b. Someone close to you can help you stop doing something that may hurt other people.

   c. A parent or teacher can show you how to change a behavior or attitude that could hurt you or another person.

   d. Sometimes we don't notice bad habits or things in our lives that we should change, but the other people in our lives can lovingly point out these things and help us get past them!

6. God uses other people to help us during hard times. Have you ever had someone help you when you were sad, afraid, or nervous about something? How did they help you?

Polka Dot Talk

2nd and 3rd Grade
Group Discussion Questions

1. God said, "It's not good for man to be alone." So he made a companion for Adam. What is a companion?

    a. A companion is a friend.

    b. It is someone who goes on a journey with you.

    c. It is someone who you share your life with.

2. God brings all kinds of special people into our lives. Tell the group about someone who is very special to you. Why is that person important to you?

3. Practice saying the theme verse together a few times. "*Treat people in the same way that you want them to treat you.*" – Luke 6:31 (CEB)

4. God gives us relationships to help us grow. Is there someone in your life who has taught you something or helped you realize something you are good at? Share it with the group!

5. Our relationships can also help "rub off the rough edges" in our lives. What does that mean?

    a. A friend can help you see something that you need to change.

    b. Someone close to you can help you stop doing something that may hurt other people.

    c. A parent or teacher can show you how to change a behavior or attitude that could hurt you or another person.

    d. Sometimes we don't notice bad habits or things in our lives that we should change, but the other people in our lives can lovingly point out these things and help us get past them!

6. God uses other people to help us during hard times. Have you ever had someone help you when you were sad, afraid, or nervous about something? How did they help you?

4th and 5th Grade
Group Discussion Questions

1. God said, "It's not good for man to be alone." So he made a companion for Adam. What is a companion?

   a. A companion is a friend.

   b. It is someone who goes on a journey with you.

   c. It is someone who you share your life with.

2. God brings all kinds of special people into our lives. Tell the group about someone who is very special to you. Why is that person important to you?

3. Practice saying the theme verse together a few times. "*Treat people in the same way that you want them to treat you.*" – Luke 6:31 (CEB)

4. God gives us relationships to help us grow. Is there someone in your life who has taught you something or helped you realize something you are good at? Share it with the group!

5. Our relationships can also help "rub off the rough edges" in our lives. What does that mean?

   a. A friend can help you see something that you need to change.

   b. Someone close to you can help you stop doing something that may hurt other people.

   c. A parent or teacher can show you how to change a behavior or attitude that could hurt you or another person.

   d. Sometimes we don't notice bad habits or things in our lives that we should change, but the other people in our lives can lovingly point out these things and help us get past them!

6. God uses other people to help us during hard times. Have you ever had someone help you when you were sad, afraid, or nervous about something? How did they help you?

Rough to Beautifully Smooth Sandpaper Art

<u>Supplies Needed:</u>

- Sandpaper (60 grit or 100 grit)
- Crayons
- White Cardstock (optional)
- Towel (optional)
- Iron (optional)
- Paper Towel or thin cloth (optional)

<u>Prep:</u>

- Cut sandpaper into 5 x 7" or 8 x 11" sizes. Size will depend upon age and skill of each girl.
- On top of each piece, write in crayon (pressing hard) the following scripture: "*As iron sharpens iron, so a friend sharpens a friend.*" – Proverbs 27:17

<u>What Should We Do Next?</u>

- Using crayons, color a picture on the sandpaper.
- Encourage the girls to draw a picture that highlights a relationship in their life that helps them grow. For example, they could draw their family, friends, pastor or teachers.
- Press hard with the crayons to get a nice layer of color.
- Each picture should cover the entire piece of sandpaper, so make sure the girls color the background too.
- **Optional – The following step can be done during group or the instructions below can be sent home to be done with a parent.**

  1. Put the sandpaper picture face up on a towel.
  2. Put a piece of white cardstock on top of the picture and a paper towel or thin cloth on top of that.

3. Using a warm iron, iron over the picture for about 15 seconds.

4. Carefully lift up the cardstock to reveal your picture. The picture will reveal a cool dot affect.

5. Look at the sandpaper art, you will notice that the crayon wax melted onto the grains of sand in the sandpaper creating a smooth, finished, sometimes sparkly effect.

6. Every piece of artwork looks better in a frame! Buy or create a cute frame for your masterpieces!

Polka Dot Plus

Weekly Challenge

Grow – Read the story of God creating Adam and Eve found in Genesis 2.

Love – Think of the people in your life who are important to you. Write them a note or just tell them how much they mean to you. You will make their day!

Act – If you notice someone who seems sad or lonely or upset, go and talk to them. Maybe they just need someone to listen and remind them that they are not alone.

Memorize – Memorize this week's theme verse.

"Treat people in the same way that you want them to treat you."

Luke 6:31 (CEB)

Parent Partner

One of the greatest life skills we, as parents, need to teach our children is how to navigate the relationships in their lives. From friendships to teachers, family scenarios to teammate relationships, our kids must navigate daily the tricky waters of relationship.

The next few weeks and months in Polka Dot Girls, your daughter will be studying what the Bible has to say about relationships. We are going to talk about being a good friend, honoring and respecting your elders and teachers, and how to navigate conflict and difficult friendships along with a number of other topics. Our goal is to fill their pretty little pink tool box chock FULL of ideas, resources, and information to help them have healthy boundaries and a Godly perspective when it comes to dealing with other people.

This week, we specifically talked about "God's Super Secret Weapon" when it comes to ANY relational scenario we may face – simply to treat others the way you would like to be treated. (Luke 6:31) This will be the foundation for all the specific topics we will cover throughout this study. (Good reminder for Moms and Dads, too!!)

We also reminded them that the relationships in our lives are special gifts that God has given us to help us grow, help rub off our rough edges, and to help us get through hard times. The people in our lives are special gifts that God has blessed us with and we should work really, really hard to make them as healthy as possible.

Kindergarten and 1st Grade
Take Home Activity Sheet

God created us to share our lives with other people. In the frames, draw and color the following pictures:

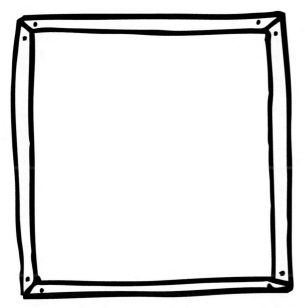

You and your parents

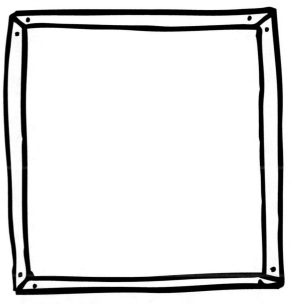

You and your favorite teacher

You and your best friend

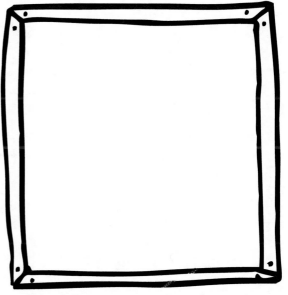

The first two companions on Earth: Adam & Eve

Fill in the missing letters to reveal the verse.

tr___ at

pe ___ ple

___ n

___ he

sa ___ e

wa ___

th___t

yo ___

wa___ t

th___ m

t___

tr___at

y___o.

– Luke 6:31 (CEB)

Polka Dot Girls ❖ Relationships

Polka Dot Plus

2nd and 3rd Grade
Take Home Activity Sheet

Find the highlighted words in each verse in the puzzle below. All scripture NIV

*"Do to **others** as you **would** have them do to you."* – Luke 6:31

*"The **LORD** God formed the man from the **dust** of the **ground** and **breathed** into his **nostrils** the breath of **life**, and the man became a **living** being."* – Genesis 2:7

*"The LORD **God** said, "It is not **good** for the man to be **alone**. I will make a **helper** suitable for him."* – Genesis 2:18

*"Wounds from a **friend** can be **trusted**, but an enemy multiplies **kisses**."* – Proverbs 27:6

*"As **iron** sharpens iron, so one man **sharpens** another."* – Proverbs 27:17

```
D D L M T B D G Y T G O L U A
R K E C K N K R W E O G N T S
O E H T E Z S O T R D S I N A
L T Y I S G U U L Z A X E L S
K I R J M U A N K A C P V C B
Y F R S X U R D S E R E H V R
B Q L O M E K T X A W F I L E
X J X O N M N I H R A I B E A
Q R N O U M S S S N E L M R T
V T L W J F O W E S S P Y N H
E A U S Q V R F O R E N L V E
S L I R T S O N E U P S U E D
L I V I N G E H D H L U S H H
C L G O O D T A Q Z O D P B U
I F Y P N O G D U S T X V D Y
```

week 1

4th and 5th Grade
Take Home Activity Sheet

Step 1: Read each verse below and find the missing word. All scripture NIV

"Do to (1) _____ as you would have them do to you." – Luke 6:31

"The LORD God formed the man from the dust of the ground and breathed into his nostrils the (2) _____ of life, and the man became a living being." – Genesis 2:7

"The LORD God said, "It is not good for the man to be (3) _____. I will make a helper suitable for him." – Genesis 2:18

"Wounds from a friend can be (4) _____, but an enemy multiplies kisses." – Proverbs 27:6

"As iron (5) _____ iron, so one man sharpens another." – Proverbs 27:17

Step 2: Fill in the missing word from each scripture above with the corresponding number.

1. ____   2. ____   5. ____

   ____   ____   ____

   ____   ____   ____

   ____   ____   4. ____   ____

   ____   ____   3. ____   ____   ____

               ____   ____

               ____   ____   ____

               ____   ____

               ____   ____

                                ____

Step 3: Complete the sentence below by copying the letters of the outlined word in Step 2 to discover what God wants us to do with our lives.

God created us to ____ ____ ____ ____ ____ our lives with other people.

25

Relationships

Friendship

WHAT'S THE POINT?
IF WE WANT TO HAVE GOOD FRIENDS, THEN WE MUST BE A GOOD FRIEND.

theme verse
"A man that hath friends must show himself friendly…"
Proverbs 18:24 (KJ21)

related bible story
Ruth and Naomi
Ruth 1

❀ Large Group Lesson ❀

There's NOTHING like a really good friend. You know, the kind that you can laugh with until your face hurts and your stomach aches. The kind that you can talk to on your very worst day and they somehow make you feel better. The kind that just KNOWS when you are super nervous about your school project and they can make you feel like everything is going to be ok.

Good friends are gifts from God. He loves to bless us with people who make our lives better. God gives us friends so we have can have fun together! He gives us friends to support and encourage us when we're going through hard times. He gives us friends to challenge us and inspire us to grow. And God gives us friends so we know we're not alone in this life.

When I think of all the friends that God has given me, I am amazed at how many of them there are and how each one brings such unique and fun things to my life. There is my friend Jessica who is SO smart – she inspires me to work hard and learn new things. My friend Dawn is such an encourager – she always sends me sweet notes and emails that make me feel good about myself. My friend Diane is so much fun – she always knows how to make me laugh. My friend Jen is so loyal – I know that I can count on her for anything. And my friend Brenda is a huge help to me – anytime I need something, she is always willing to lend me a hand.

Our friendships are something that we should take really good care of. The Bible tells that if we want to HAVE good friends, then we must BE a good friend. Proverbs 18:24 says, "*A man that hath friends must show himself friendly…*" (KJ21) This means that we need to take the time and effort to make sure that we are being a good friend.

Remember God's super-secret weapon for relationships?!?? Treat other people the way you want to be treated! So you should BE the kind of friend that you would want to have!!!

So, what are some ways that we can be a good friend?

⇒ 1. Be a LOYAL friend.

What does it mean to be loyal? A loyal friend is someone you can count on. It's someone who you KNOW will be there for you no matter what. It is someone who has your back no matter what you may face.

Being loyal means that your friends know that they can count on you. If something is going on in their lives, they know that you will be there for them. If other people are saying bad things about you, a loyal friend will stick up for you. No matter what, you are confident that they have your back.

Have you ever had a really loyal friend? Someone who was always there for you no matter what? There is nothing quite as comforting as knowing that there is someone sticking up for you. It is such a good feeling to know that there are people who will always be there for you and who are willing to stand up to other people for you.

Have you ever had a friend who wasn't loyal? The kind of friend who will be your friend one day and then the next day they will be mad at you? Or maybe you have had a friend who says, "I'm not going to be your friend anymore" if you don't do what they want you to do. Loyal friends don't say "I'm not going to be your friend anymore." Loyal friends may have disagreements, but they never threaten to take away their friendship.

I remember a friend that I had when I was younger who was NOT a very loyal friend. It seemed like she was always mad at me for one reason or another. I was never totally sure that she wasn't talking about me behind my back. It took me a long time to realize it, but she wasn't a very good friend to me. After a lot of tears and frustration, I finally decided to spend my time on the friends who were loyal to me. I was still kind to her, and I would still be her friend, but I learned that she just couldn't be a really close friend to me because I couldn't count on her to be there for me.

Maybe you haven't been a very loyal friend. Maybe you haven't been consistent with the friends in your life. Today is the day that you can start being a loyal friend. Decide that you are going to be there for your friends no matter what. When you get frustrated with them, talk it through, but never threaten to take your friendship away. Fill your friends with the confidence that comes from knowing that you'll be there for them.

God wants you to be a LOYAL friend. Proverbs 17:7 says, "*A friend is always loyal.*" If you want to be a good friend, be a loyal friend.

The second way we can be a good friend is to:

⟹ 2. Be an encourager

Have you ever had a friend in your life that made you feel like you could do anything? You know, the kind that tells you to GO FOR IT and cheers you on along the way? An encouraging friend is someone who helps you believe in yourself. They are the friends who tell you all the things you are good at. They compliment you and are proud of you when you do well at something.

Sarah had the most encouraging friend EVER! Her name was Abby. No matter what she was doing, Abby was always there for her. When Sarah decided to audition for the jazz band at school, she was SO nervous she could hardly stand it. But Abby called her and TOTALLY encouraged her. She said, "Sarah, you are SO good – you are going to do AWESOME at your audition. I know you are going to be amazing!" Sarah couldn't believe how much stronger she felt after her friend spoke encouraging words to her.

1 Thessalonians 5:11 says, *"So encourage each other and build each other up."* God wants us to make each other feel better about ourselves. We should be pointing out all the GOOD things about our friends and encouraging them!

But sometimes it can be hard to be encouraging. Why is that? Sometimes, when our friends do really well at something, we can feel jealous. Or when our friends do something really amazing, it makes us feel bad about ourselves because WE didn't do something as amazing as them. But those are all silly reasons not to encourage our friends, right?!

The truth is, just because someone else is successful doesn't mean that WE won't be successful too! Seeing our friends do well should be something that fills us with joy, not jealousy. Helping our friends feel better about themselves is an awesome thing to do!

ILLUSTRATION:

You will need 2 candles, a lighter and two helpers. Have each girl hold a candle.

Now, when we encourage each other and cheer each other on, it's like we are lighting each other's candles.

Light the first girl's candle.

Now, I want you to say something encouraging to your friend here and light her candle.

Have the girl share something encouraging and light the other candle.

Now, when she lit her friend's candle, did anything happen to her light? Is her flame any smaller? Did her light go out when she shared her fire with her friend"

NO! When we encourage our friends, when we hope for the best for them, when we tell them how amazing and awesome they are, it doesn't take anything away from us. When your friends succeed, it doesn't mean that YOU won't be success- ful. When you light someone else's candle with your kind and encouraging words, your light stays just as bright. And now there are two of you lighting the world instead of just one!

Be an encourager. When you notice a friend doing something well, tell them! When someone is nervous about trying something new, tell them that you believe in them and they can do it! Be your friend's biggest supporter and cheerleader.

Encourage each other. Live in harmony and peace.
Then the God of love and peace will be with you.

2 Corinthians 13:11

So, be a good friend by being loyal, encouraging, and lastly,

➡ 3. Don't be a selfish friend.

Oh my, it can be **SO** easy to think about the things **WE** want! The things **WE** want to play. The things **WE** want to do. The things **WE** want our friends to do. The things **WE DON'T** want our friends to do.

But a good friend doesn't just think about the things **WE** want, we think about our friends! Philippians 2:3 says, *"Don't be selfish; don't try to impress others. Be humble, thinking of others as better than yourselves."* This means that we aren't supposed to only think about the things **WE** want, but we should think about our friends too!

There is a story in the Bible about a girl who did something **AMAZINGLY** unselfish for her friend. Her name was Ruth, and she was a very good friend to her mother-in-law Naomi. All of Naomi's family had died, so she decided to move away from where she was living, back to the home of her ancestors. Her daughter-in-law, Ruth, decided to go with her so she wouldn't be alone.

Now this was a **HUGE** deal. Ruth would have to leave all her family and friends and move to a new country where she didn't know anyone! But she knew that her mother-in-law would really need her, and so she was willing to go with her. She thought about Naomi's feelings and needs far above her own. In Ruth 1:16 she says, *"Wherever you go, I will go; wherever you live, I will live. Your people will be my people and your God will be my God."*

I can imagine that it would have been a difficult decision for Ruth. But she thought about what was best for Naomi and how she could help and support her instead of what might be easiest for her. Ruth was a very unselfish friend.

God wants you to think about other people's feelings – not just your own. He wants you to consider ways that you can encourage and bless the people in your life – not just think about what **YOU** want all the time.

Don't you think it would be $\mathcal{SO}$ cool if we all could simply be the kind of friend that we would want to have? A friend who is loyal no matter what? A friend who encourages us and cheers us on? And a friend who isn't selfish but thinks of what is best for the other people in their lives?

I want those kinds of friends. And I want to be that kind of friend.

Closing Prayer: *Dear God. Thank you for the gift of friendship. I pray that you will help me be the best friend possible. Help me be loyal, encouraging, and unselfish to the friends in my life. I love you, Amen.*

Kindergarten and 1st Grade Group Discussion Questions

1. Do you have a really good friend? Tell the group one thing about your special friend and why they are such a good friend to you!

2. The Bible tells us that if we want to HAVE good friends, then we must BE a good friend. Practice saying the theme verse together. "*A man that hath friends must show himself friendly...*" – Proverbs 18:24 (KJ21)

3. What does it mean to be a loyal friend?

    a. You stick up for that person

    b. You are there for them no matter what

    c. You have their back

    d. You want the very best for them

    e. You are always there for them

    f. You don't say "I'm not going to be your friend anymore."

4. Have you ever had a friend encourage you? How did it make you feel?

    a. Strong

    b. Like I could do anything

    c. Confident

    d. Happy

    e. Loved

5. God doesn't want us to be a selfish friend. What are some ways that you can think of others instead of yourself?

    a. Letting your friend pick what you are going to play

    b. Taking turns

    c. Not demanding your own way all the time.

    d. Thinking of what your friend would want instead of only thinking about what YOU want.

Polka Dot Talk

2nd and 3rd Grade Group Discussion Questions

1. Do you have a really good friend? Tell the group one thing about your special friend and why they are such a good friend to you!

2. The Bible tells us that if we want to HAVE good friends, then we must BE a good friend. Practice saying the theme verse together. "*A man that hath friends must show himself friendly...*" – Proverbs 18:24 (KJ21)

3. What does it mean to be a loyal friend?

   a. You stick up for that person

   b. You are there for them no matter what

   c. You have their back

   d. You want the very best for them

   e. You are always there for them

   f. You don't say "I'm not going to be your friend anymore."

   g. You don't talk about them behind their back.

4. Have you ever had a friend encourage you? How did it make you feel?

   a. Strong

   b. Like I could do anything

   c. Confident

   d. Loved

   e. Brave

5. God doesn't want us to be a selfish friend. What are some ways that you can think of others instead of yourself?

   a. Letting your friend pick what you are going to do

   b. Taking turns

   c. Not demanding your own way all the time.

   d. Thinking of what your friend would want instead of only thinking about what YOU want.

   e. Being considerate of your friend's feelings

4th and 5th Grade
Group Discussion Questions

1. Do you have a really good friend? Tell the group one thing about your special friend and why they are such a good friend to you!

2. The Bible tells us that if we want to HAVE good friends, then we must BE a good friend. Practice saying the theme verse together. *"A man that hath friends must show himself friendly..."* – Proverbs 18:24 KJ21

3. What does it mean to be a loyal friend?

   a. You stick up for that person

   b. You are there for them no matter what

   c. You have their back

   d. You want the very best for them

   e. You are always there for them

   f. You don't say "I'm not going to be your friend anymore."

   g. You don't talk about them behind their back.

4. Have you ever had a friend encourage you? How did it make you feel?

   a. Strong

   b. Like I could do anything

   c. Confident

   d. Loved

   e. Brave

5. God doesn't want us to be a selfish friend. What are some ways that you can think of others instead of yourself?

a. Letting your friend pick what you are going to do

b. Taking turns

c. Not demanding your own way all the time.

d. Thinking of what your friend would want instead of only thinking about what YOU want.

e. Being considerate of your friend's feelings

Chenille Pipe Cleaner Friendship Bracelets
(Recommended for K-2nd grade)

<u>Supplies Needed:</u>
- Cardstock
- Friendship Notecard Template
- Chenille Stems (craft pipe cleaner) – two per girl.
- 6 mm Pony Beads
- Scissors
- Bells or funky beads (optional)

<u>Prep:</u>
- Print the template on cardstock
- Cut the template so each girl will have one notecard to give to her friend with the bracelet.

<u>What Should We Do Next?</u>
- Wrap the chenille stem around each girl's wrist.
- Cut it a few inches longer than needed.
- String the beads on the stem, leaving 1-2" at the end.
- Leave enough stem after the last bead to twist with the other end and secure.
- Tuck the ends of the stem into the beads so that the sharp end doesn't poke out.
- Repeat steps for the second bracelet.
- Complete the friendship card.
- Each girl will keep one bracelet for themselves and give the other bracelet to their friend with the notecard.

Dear _____,

You mean the world to me! I made this bracelet for you. I have one just like it. Every time I wear it I will think of you and how grateful I am that you are my friend!

Love,

_____

Dear _____,

You mean the world to me! I made this bracelet for you. I have one just like it. Every time I wear it I will think of you and how grateful I am that you are my friend!

Love,

_____

Dear _____,

You mean the world to me! I made this bracelet for you. I have one just like it. Every time I wear it I will think of you and how grateful I am that you are my friend!

Love,

_____

Dear _____,

You mean the world to me! I made this bracelet for you. I have one just like it. Every time I wear it I will think of you and how grateful I am that you are my friend!

Love,

_____

Ribbon Friendship Bracelet

(Recommended for 3rd-5th grade)

Supplies Needed:
- Metallic jewelry elastic (can be found at any craft store)
- Large 20 mm sized beads in the following colors:

  Blue = Loyalty/Trust   **Orange** = Encouragement

  Purple = Creativity   **Clear/White** = Jesus

  Red = Laughter   **Hot Pink** = Fun

  Green = Make up your own special meaning
- Satin Ribbon
- Scissors
- Friendship Notecard Template
- Cardstock

Prep:
- Print template onto cardstock so each girl has one card to give to a friend.
- Cut two 12" lengths of elastic per girl.
- Cut two 6" pieces of satin ribbon per girl.

What Should We Do Next?
- Fold over the 12" length of elastic to create a double 6" piece.
- Thread beads onto the elastic one by one.
- Take two ends and tie together fairly tight into a knot. Triple knot to secure it.
- Tie a bow over the elastic knot with the satin ribbon.
- Repeat the steps above and make an identical bracelet for a friend.
- Complete the friendship card
- Encourage a friend by giving them the card and bracelet!

Dear _____,

You mean the world to me! I made this bracelet for you. I have one just like it. Every time I wear it I will think of you and how grateful I am that you are my friend!

Each bead has a special meaning:

Blue = Loyalty/Trust   Orange = Encouragement

Purple = Creativity   Clear/White = Jesus

Red = Laughter   Hot Pink = Fun

Green = _____

Love,
_____

Dear _____,

You mean the world to me! I made this bracelet for you. I have one just like it. Every time I wear it I will think of you and how grateful I am that you are my friend!

Each bead has a special meaning:

Blue = Loyalty/Trust   Orange = Encouragement

Purple = Creativity   Clear/White = Jesus

Red = Laughter   Hot Pink = Fun

Green = _____

Love,

Dear _____,

You mean the world to me! I made this bracelet for you. I have one just like it. Every time I wear it I will think of you and how grateful I am that you are my friend!

Each bead has a special meaning:

Blue = Loyalty/Trust   Orange = Encouragement

Purple = Creativity   Clear/White = Jesus

Red = Laughter   Hot Pink = Fun

Green = _____

Love,
_____

Dear _____,

You mean the world to me! I made this bracelet for you. I have one just like it. Every time I wear it I will think of you and how grateful I am that you are my friend!

Each bead has a special meaning:

Blue = Loyalty/Trust   Orange = Encouragement

Purple = Creativity   Clear/White = Jesus

Red = Laughter   Hot Pink = Fun

Green = _____

Love,

Polka Dot Plus

Weekly Challenge

Grow – Read the story of Ruth and Naomi in Ruth chapter 1.

Love – Think of a way you can encourage a friend this week. Send a note, make a phone call, or say something to let your friend know you believe in her!

Act – Do one thing this week to practice being an unselfish friend. Maybe let your friend choose what you do, let her pick first when you're sharing a treat, or simply think of what she would like before you think of what YOU would like.

Memorize – Memorize this week's theme verse.

"A man that hath friends must show himself friendly..."
Proverbs 18:24 (KJ21)

Parent Partner

This week our **Polka Dot Girls** learned what the Bible has to say about being a good friend. Once again, we reminded them that they should become the kind of friend that THEY would want to have!

We specifically discussed being a friend who is loyal. We want to encourage the girls to have each other's backs. We want to teach them to avoid the all – too – prevalent "I won't be your friend anymore if you don't do what I want you to do" attitude. Praying hard for this one!!!

We also taught them to be an encouraging friend. We want our girls to cheer each other on and not be afraid to hope for the best in our friends. Our friends should be our biggest supporters and greatest encouragers.

And lastly, we talked about being an unselfish friend. Not to only think of themselves and the things THEY want, but to be mindful of their friends' feelings, needs, and emotions. If we can instill in them an awareness of the needs of those around them, then they will be the kind of friend that God designed them to be!

Polka Dot Plus

Kindergarten and 1st Grade Take Home Activity Sheet

Draw a picture of you and your best friend!

Write the word *friend* in the blank spaces to complete the following scriptures.

Godly people are careful about the _____s they choose.
– Proverbs 12:26 NIRV

A _____ loves at all times. He is there to help when trouble comes.
– Proverbs 17:17 NIRV

*Perfume and incense bring joy to your heart. And a _____ is
sweeter when he gives you honest advice.* – Proverbs 27:9 NIRV

*Agree with each other. Don't be proud. Be willing to be a _____ of
people who aren't considered important. Don't think that you are better than others.*
– Romans 12:16 NIRV

2nd and 3rd Grade
Take Home Activity Sheet

Don't be afraid to cheer your friends on. We should be their biggest supporters and greatest encouragers.

In the Pom Poms below write the name of each your friends and one thing you love about her. Encourage her this week by sharing what you wrote.

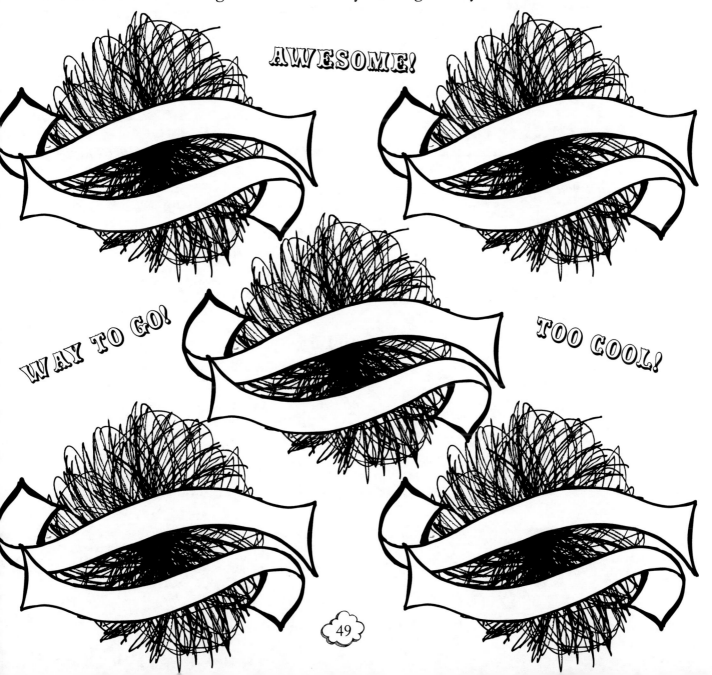

Read the following scriptures about friendship in your Bible and find the missing word. All scripture NIV.

A friend _____ at all times... – Proverbs 17:17

Perfume and incense bring _____ to the heart, and the

pleasantness of one's friend springs from his earnest counsel. – Proverbs 27:9

Live in harmony with one another. Do not be _____, but be

willing to associate with people of low position. Do not be _____.

– Romans 12:16

Therefore _____ one another and build each other up, just

as in fact you are doing. – 1 Thessalonians 5:11

Do nothing out of _____ ambition or vain conceit, but in

humility consider others better than yourselves. – Philippians 2:3

Word List

encourage	conceited	joy
loves	selfish	proud

4th and 5th Grade
Take Home Activity Sheet

Things about us! Fill out this survey with a friend.

Question	Answer: Me	Answer: You
1. Favorite food		
2. Favorite movie		
3. Favorite book		
4. If you could be an animal, what would it be?		
5. What word best describes you?		
6. If you could go anywhere in the world, where would you go?		
7. Name one great thing about your family		
8. Favorite season		
9. Favorite singer		
10. What are you scared of?		

Question	Answer: Me	Answer: You
11. If you won a million dollars, what would you do with it?		
12. Favorite animal		
13. If you could change your name, what would it be?		
14. What do you like better? a. Candy or chips b. Singing or dancing c. Dogs or cats d. Sports or music e. Shopping or reading f. Board games or computer games g. Camping or hotels h. Sweat pants or jeans i. On stage or behind the scenes j. Winter or summer k. Hot Chocolate or lemonade l. Biking or skateboarding		
15. What will I be doing in 10 years?		
16. Will we be friends forever?		

Ruth & Naomi: Friends Forever!

Read Ruth 1:16-18 NIV in the Bible and find the missing word. Find those same words in the word search puzzle.

"¹⁶But _____ replied, "Don't urge me to _____ you or to turn back from you. Where you _____ I will go, and where you _____ I will stay. Your _____ will be my people and your _____ my God. ¹⁷Where you _____ I will die, and there I will be _____. May the _____ deal with me, be it ever so severely, if anything but death _____ you and me." ¹⁸When _____ realized that Ruth was _____ to go with her, she stopped urging her."

```
S  E  P  A  R  A  T  E  S  E  O  B
O  L  N  G  B  N  I  O  V  L  L  U
G  P  O  S  T  A  Y  H  D  I  E  R
N  O  D  R  E  O  L  T  O  E  A  I
T  E  D  P  D  M  I  U  M  E  V  E
L  P  D  E  N  I  M  R  E  T  E  D
```

Word List

Ruth	leave	go	Naomi
stay	people	God	determined
buried	Lord	separates	die

My Family

WHAT'S THE POINT?
HONOR YOUR PARENTS, BE KIND TO YOUR FAMILY, AND STICK TOGETHER!

theme verse

I pray that the Lord will let your family and your descendants always grow strong.

Psalm 115:14 CEV

related bible story

Joab and Abishai

I Chronicles 19

❋ Large Group Lesson ❋

They see your best and they know your worst. They are the people who mean the most to you, and the people who can drive you nutty the fastest. The people who you would stick up for you to anyone, anywhere, over anything – but also the people who you spend the most time fighting, arguing, and getting crazy mad at. They are the ones who can make you feel the best about yourself, but sometimes they are the people who can say things that make you feel bad, too. Who are these loony people?

Your family.

We talked earlier in this book about the fact that God gives us people in our world to walk through our lives together. And there is NO one closer to us on our journey than our families. They are the ones we live with and spend the most time around.

God gives us families to help us in countless ways. Do you remember being a baby? Really? I don't either. But your parents were the ones who cared for you when you were a baby. They changed your diapers (ick!) and mushed up your food (gross!) and made sure you were taken well care of. As you grew older, they showed you how to do things, taught you all the stuff you needed to learn, and made sure that you were always safe.

And now, your Mom and Dad do their best to teach you all the things you need to learn in order to become the best person you can possibly be. They are not perfect, and will make lots of mistakes, but they love you and want the best for you… even if sometimes they don't do everything perfectly.

And then we have other people in our family! We have brothers and sisters and cousins and grandparents and lots of other people who are all a part of our families. Some people have really big families – and some people have really small families. Some families live really close and spend a lot of time together, and some families don't really spend much time together at all. No matter what your family may look like, God has some instructions for you as to how you should deal with the people in your family.

First of all, God gives us some very important instructions when it comes to how we treat our parents. It is this:

➡ 1. We need to honor our parents.

There are quite a few places in the Bible where we find this very specific direction. Ephesians 6:1-3 says, "*Children, obey your parents because you belong to the Lord, for this is the right thing to do. Honor your father and mother. This is the first commandment with a promise: If you honor your father and mother, things will go well for you, and you will have a long life on the earth.*"

What does is mean to HONOR our parents? Honoring someone means respecting them. It means obeying them and doing the things that they ask of you. It means speaking to them in a way that isn't sassy or rude. When you honor someone, you are thanking them for the special role that they play in your life.

You see, God has given you to your parents as their responsibility. When you honor them by doing the things they ask of you, speaking in a way that is respectful, and having an attitude of appreciation towards them, you are honoring the role God has given them in your life. So, when you honor your parents, you are really honoring God!

I know that sometimes it can be hard to honor your parents. There are moments when they frustrate us. There are times we simply don't want to do what they say. And sometimes, we don't understand why they want us to do the things they want us to do. But no matter what, you need to HONOR them.

Not only does this please God when we act that way, but there is a reward for us when we follow this very important rule! Actually, this is the first commandment in the Bible that comes with a promise. God makes a deal with us. He says, "If you will honor your parents and treat them with respect, then I am going to help things to go well for you." I think that's a pretty good deal!

You need to work really hard to honor your parents. When you feel like ignoring what they tell you to do, remember that God wants you to honor them by obeying. When you start to say something sassy, stop yourself and remember that God wants you to speak respectfully to your parents. When you are tempted to treat your parents poorly or have a bad attitude, ask God to help you honor your parents even when it is difficult.

Sometimes we can think to ourselves, "Well, I'm frustrated with my Mom and Dad, so I don't have to honor them." You know what? God doesn't tell us that we only honor our parents if we like the things they are telling us to do. He doesn't tell us that we only have to honor our parents when we feel like it. The Bible tells us that it is our responsibility to keep our attitudes respectful and honoring to our parents. It doesn't depend on their behavior toward us, or only if we feel like they have earned it. God wants you to honor your parents, no matter what.

Just so You Know

There are a lot of situations in which it can be really difficult to honor your parents. Sometimes your parents can go through a hard time and may treat you in a way that they shouldn't. If you are ever scared by something your Mom or Dad are doing, it's really important that you talk to someone about it. Share your concerns with a teacher, another family member, a friend or even your pastor. When you seek help for your Mom or Dad when they need it, you are honoring them in a really special way. You are respecting them enough to get help – and God will be really, really proud of you.

So, God wants you to **HONOR** your parents.

Another thing that God wants you to do is:

⇒ 2. Be KIND to your family.

Kindness, hmmmm. Seems easy enough, right? Of course we all know that we should be kind to each other. But sometimes it can be really hard to be kind to the people closest to us.

Heather has a brother named Joe. Heather loves her brother, but she's not so sure how much she likes him. He can really, really get on her nerves. Sometimes, he does things just to bother her and no matter what she says, he just won't stop. After a while, Heather finds herself **EXPLODING** at her brother. She screams and yells and sometimes she even wants to hit the little bugger!

What is so crazy is that Heather would **NEVER** think of screaming or yelling or wanting to hit one of her friends! Even if they made her super mad, she wouldn't think of treating a friend that way.

But sometimes we treat our families way different than we would ever treat our friends. We are a lot less cautious about the things we say and do with the people closest to us. It's easy to forget that our brothers and sisters and other family members have feelings just like our friends!

God wants you to be kind to your family. Even if they are driving you crazy. Even if you are so frustrated you just want to scream! Even if they are not kind to you. 2 Timothy 2:24 says, "*A servant of the Lord must not quarrel but must be kind to everyone, be able to teach, and be patient with difficult people.*" (Yes, your little brother will fall into the category of "difficult people" sometimes!)

You must be kind to your family. Don't say mean things to your brother or sister. Don't tease them. Don't make fun of them. Don't react when they are trying to get you angry. When you feel like you are going to lose it and say something UNKIND, stop yourself and remember that God wants us to be kind to one another. Maybe you'll need to walk away and take a few minutes to calm yourself down. Maybe you need to go talk to your Mom or Dad about the situation. Or maybe you just need to smile at them and tell them you love them.

You will never regret the moments when you are kind to other people. Even if they don't deserve it, you will know that you made the right choice in choosing kindness.

And the last way God wants you to treat your family, is to:

➡ 3. Stick together.

Remember when we talked about loyalty? Being loyal means you stand by someone no matter what. And there is no place that loyalty is more important than among your family members.

God didn't make a mistake when He put you in the family you are in. He did it for a reason. He gave you your family so you would have someone to walk through life with you… to help you, support you, and have your back.

There is a story in the Bible about two brothers who had each other's backs. Joab was the leader of the army for King David. He had to fight all kinds of bad guys

who were trying to destroy the nation of Israel. Joab was facing a tough situation. There were people ahead of him wanting to fight him… and there were people behind him who wanted to fight him. He was surrounded! So you know what he did? He called on his brother to help him. I Chronicles 19:10-13 says, "*When Joab saw that he had two fronts to fight, before and behind, he took his pick of the best of Israel and deployed them to confront the Arameans. The rest of the army he put under the command of Abishai, **his brother**, and deployed them to deal with the Ammonites. Then he said, 'If the Arameans are too much for me, you help me; and if the Ammonites prove too much for you, I'll come and help you. Courage!'*"

Did you read that? These brothers had each others backs! If one of them needed help – they knew that the other one would be there for them. If they were in trouble, their family would fight for them. Joab could confidently go into battle knowing that his brother was right by his side.

We know in our hearts that we should be there for our families. But sometimes we can get so busy with all the things we are doing – our friends, our activities, and the things we are involved in-that we can forget that part of our job is to be there for the people in our families.

Maybe your brother or sister is having a hard time and they don't have anyone to talk to. Would they feel comfortable coming to you with their problems? Would they feel like you would listen to them or help them? Or would they feel like you would tell them to leave you alone so you could do other things?

If your Mom was having a really busy week and she was totally over-whelmed, could she count on you to help her with the chores around the house and to maybe help clean up? Or would you react with a million excuses as to why it's not fair that you have to help.

Families stick together. They help each other out. They work together as a team to help each person succeed. Our families are a team. When we only think about ourselves and what we want and what we are doing, we are never going to get anywhere. But when we decide to work together, and think of ways that we can help each other out, our families will grow stronger and we will all be stronger individuals too!

ILLUSTRATION: 8 Legged Race

Have 4 girls come up on stage and stand in a line. Tie their legs together as if they were in a three legged race. (the two girls in the middle will have both their legs tied and the girls on the end will have just one leg tied.)

Now, tell the girls to walk across the stage randomly. As they each try and walk normally, they will probably stumble and fall.

THEN, tell the girls that they need to work together to walk across the stage. Tell them to start with their right foot and then give verbal cues as to which foot to step with (left – right – left – right…)

"Do you see how that worked? When they each were just trying to do their own thing without thinking of what the other person was doing, they couldn't get anywhere! But when they stopped, and worked together, they made a lot of progress!"

Our families are a gift from God. He blessed you with people who love you, care about you, and want to help you do the very best you can. Don't take your family for granted… but do your best to treat them with all the love and respect you can. Yes… even your annoying little brother.

Closing Prayer: *Dear God, thank you for my family. I know that they are a special treasure from you, and I am so grateful for them. Show me ways that I can honor my Mom and Dad. Help me show kindness to my family members, even when it's hard. And teach me ways that I can support my family and help us work together as a team. I love you, Jesus. Amen.*

Kindergarten and 1st Grade Group Discussion Questions

1. God gives our families to us as a gift. Share one thing that you love about your family with the girls in your group.

2. What does it mean to honor your parents?

   a. You respect them.

   b. You don't talk sassy to them.

   c. You listen to the things they say to you.

   d. You obey them when they ask you to do something

   e. You have a good attitude towards them.

3. If we honor our parents, God makes a promise to us. What is the promise?

   a. If we honor our parents, things will go well for us. (Ephesians 6:1-3 "*Children, obey your parents because you belong to the Lord, for this is the right thing to do. Honor your father and mother. This is the first commandment with a promise: If you honor your father and mother, things will go well for you, and you will have a long life on the earth.*")

4. Another thing that God wants us to do is to treat our family with kindness. Why do you think it is so hard to be kind to our family sometimes?

   a. They get on our nerves.

   b. We spend so much time with them.

   c. We live with them!

   d. Sometimes it can be hard to remember that they have feelings just like your friends.

   e. They can be mean to us.

5. What are some specific ways you can be kind to your family?

   a. Not yelling at them

   b. Being kind in the things you say to them

   c. Treating them nicely – even if they're not being nice to you.

   d. Helping them with things when they need help

   e. Listening to them

   f. Doing nice things for them to show them you care about them.

6. Another way we can be a good member of a family is by sticking together. What does it mean to "have someone's back?"

   a. It means we watch out for each other.

   b. We take care of each other.

   c. We help each other when we need help.

   d. We stick up for each other.

   e. We work together as a team.

Polka Dot Talk

2nd and 3rd Grade Group Discussion Questions

1. God gives our families to us as a gift. Share one thing that you love about your family with the girls in your group.

2. What does it mean to honor your parents?

   a. You respect them.

   b. You don't talk sassy to them.

   c. You listen to the things they say to you.

   d. You obey them when they ask you to do something

   e. You have a good attitude towards them.

3. If we honor our parents, God makes a promise to us. What is the promise?

   a. If we honor our parents, things will go well for us. (Ephesians 6:1-3 *"Children, obey your parents because you belong to the Lord, for this is the right thing to do. Honor your father and mother. This is the first commandment with a promise: If you honor your father and mother, things will go well for you, and you will have a long life on the earth."*)

4. Another thing that God wants us to do is to treat our family with kindness. Why do you think it is so hard to be kind to our family sometimes?

   a. They get on our nerves.

   b. We spend so much time with them.

   c. We live with them!

   d. Sometimes it can be hard to remember that they have feelings just like your friends.

   e. They can be mean to us.

5. What are some specific ways you can be kind to your family?

    a. Not yelling at them

    b. Being kind in the things you say to them

    c. Treating them nicely – even if they're not being nice to you.

    d. Helping them with things when they need help

    e. Listening to them

    f. Doing nice things for them to show them you care about them.

6. Another way we can be a good member of a family is by sticking together. What does it mean to "have someone's back?"

    a. It means we watch out for each other.

    b. We take care of each other.

    c. We help each other when we need help.

    d. We stick up for each other.

    e. We work together as a team.

4th and 5th Grade
Group Discussion Questions

1. God gives our families to us as a gift. Share one thing that you love about your family with the girls in your group.

2. What does it mean to honor your parents?

   a. You respect them.

   b. You don't talk sassy to them.

   c. You listen to the things they say to you.

   d. You obey them when they ask you to do something

   e. You have a good attitude towards them.

3. If we honor our parents, God makes a promise to us. What is the promise?

   a. If we honor our parents, things will go well for us. (Ephesians 6:1-3 *"Children, obey your parents because you belong to the Lord, for this is the right thing to do. Honor your father and mother. This is the first commandment with a promise: If you honor your father and mother, things will go well for you, and you will have a long life on the earth."*)

4. Another thing that God wants us to do is to treat our family with kindness. Why do you think it is so hard to be kind to our family sometimes?

   a. They get on our nerves.

   b. We spend so much time with them.

   c. We live with them!

   d. Sometimes it can be hard to remember that they have feelings just like your friends.

   e. They can be mean to us.

5. What are some specific ways you can be kind to your family?

   a. Not yelling at them

   b. Being kind in the things you say to them

   c. Treating them nicely – even if they're not being nice to you.

   d. Helping them with things when they need help

   e. Listening to them

   f. Doing nice things for them to show them you care about them.

6. Another way we can be a good member of a family is by sticking together. What does it mean to "have someone's back?"

   a. It means we watch out for each other.

   b. We take care of each other.

   c. We help each other when we need help.

   d. We stick up for each other.

   e. We work together as a team.

Birds of a Feather Stick Together Family Tree

<u>Supplies Needed:</u>
- Family Tree Template
- White Cardstock
- Markers/Crayons
- Glue sticks (optional)
- Glitter (optional)
- Paper Plate (optional)

<u>Prep:</u>
- Copy Family Tree template onto white cardstock.

<u>What Should We Do Next?</u>
- Write the name of family members under each bird.
- Color the tree and birds.
- To add a little sparkle to the tree and/or birds, rub glue from the glue stick onto the picture and sprinkle some glitter over the glue.
- Shake off the extra glitter onto a paper plate.
- Encourage the girls to frame their picture and hang it on a wall as a reminder that their family is a blessing from God!

My Family

"I pray that the Lord will let your family and your descendants always grow strong."
Psalm 115:14 CEV

Polka Dot Plus

Weekly Challenge

Grow – Read the story of Joab and Abishai in I Chronicles 19.

Love – Think of some things about your family that you are thankful for. Write a note to some of your family members telling them why you are glad God gave them to you.

Act – Practice being kind to your family. When you get frustrated or upset with someone, choose to respond in kindness instead of anger and frustration.

Memorize – Memorize this week's theme verse.

"I pray that the Lord will let your family and your descendants always grow strong."
Psalm 115:14 CEV

Parent Partner

This week we talked to our polka Dot Girls about family. No matter what your home situation looks like, we all need to be purposeful in how we treat the people closet to us. The truth is that sometimes the people who we are closest to are the ones with whom we struggle with the most. We want our girls to have healthy relationships with their family members and we want to see your families vital and strong!

We shared with the girls that God wants them to honor their parents. God is very clear that we are to treat our parents with honor, respect and a good attitude. One way that you can help them with this is to be purposeful about maintaining a position of authority in your home. Now, I'm not saying that you need to be unapproachable or authoritative in a negative way. But there are times that it is easy to get lazy in our role and take on more of the role of friend instead of parent. God has placed a very specific structure in place when it comes to our families. YOU are supposed to be in charge. YOU are supposed to be leading and teaching your children. YOU are supposed to be guiding their choices, putting up boundaries, and setting high expectations for your children.

It can be really hard for them to honor you when you treat them as a peer. God has made their responsibility very clear – and therefore your expectation is clear as well. Be honorable. Be respectable. Don't let them get away with things they shouldn't be getting away with. Don't put them in a position where they need to be the grown up. Take the position that God has given you as the leaders of your household. If you are unsure how to do this, ask God for wisdom and He will graciously grant you all the wisdom you need.

Kindergarten and 1st Grade Take Home Activity Sheet

2 Timothy 2:24 says "*A servant of the Lord must not quarrel but must* BE *kind to everyone,* BE *able to teach, and* BE *patient with difficult people.*"

With a friend or family member, color the bee and create an awesome scene with your best doodles!

Fill in the blanks with the word KIND. Look up each scripture verse in your Bible. All scripture NIV.

"Love is patient, love is _____. It does not envy, it does not boast, it is not proud." – 1 Corinthians 13:4

"But the fruit of the Spirit is love, joy, peace, patience, _____ness, goodness, faithfulness…" – Galatians 5:22

"Be _____ and compassionate to one another, forgiving each other, just as in Christ, God forgave you." – Ephesians 4:32

"Make sure that nobody pays back wrong for wrong, but always try to be _____ to each other and to everyone else."

– 1 Thessalonians 5:15

2nd and 3rd Grade
Take Home Activity Sheet

God gives us people in our world to walk through our lives together. And there is NO one closer to us on our journey than our families.

Step 1: Read 1 Chronicles 19

Step 2: Find the words from the story in the Word Search Puzzle.

```
I  P  A  R  A  S  Y  R  T  H  A  T  T  H  G
E  R  P  T  S  S  E  N  D  N  I  K  P  O  P
T  O  P  L  O  S  O  L  R  D  W  A  D  A  I
Y  N  R  R  P  G  L  K  C  I  T  S  R  J  L
L  O  E  E  A  L  E  E  T  I  Y  E  O  O  U
I  H  C  M  R  Y  F  T  E  A  N  A  M  I  L
M  T  I  O  D  Y  A  N  H  T  B  O  N  D  Y
A  Y  A  B  O  N  C  U  S  E  R  D  R  T  E
F  S  T  E  C  E  A  E  N  D  R  A  L  H  N
T  S  E  Y  A  L  W  M  A  Y  S  A  G  R  C
A  B  I  S  H  A  I  O  M  W  Y  S  T  R  O
N  G  L  I  E  J  B  C  K  O  D  O  D  S  M
E  P  S  K  S  M  X  R  L  O  C  E  I  G  Q
N  S  X  Q  B  Z  W  O  F  X  A  M  J  W  H
Q  M  B  B  M  P  X  E  M  B  R  V  Q  G  K
```

WORD LIST

Abishai
commandment
kindness
patience
together

Joab
family
loyalty
pray

appreciate
God
obey
respect

Chronicles
honor
parents
stick

4th and 5th Grade
Take Home Activity Sheet

No matter what your family may look like, God has some instructions for you as to how you should deal with the people in your family.

Step 1: Unscramble the following words and put the letters in the box beneath the scrambled word.

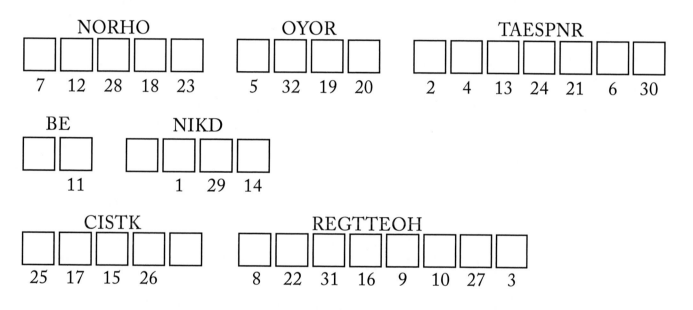

NORHO
7 12 28 18 23

OYOR
5 32 19 20

TAESPNR
2 4 13 24 21 6 30

BE
11

NIKD
1 29 14

CISTK
25 17 15 26

REGTTEOH
8 22 31 16 9 10 27 3

Step 2: Copy the letters (from the numbered cells above to the cells below with the same number) to reveal God's Word.

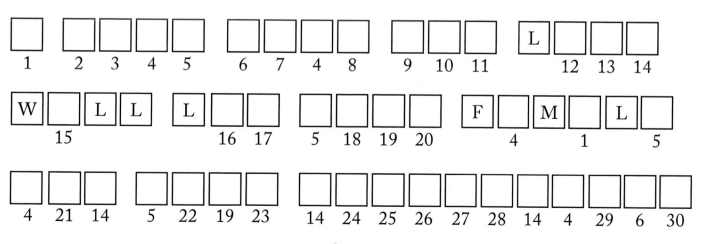

1 2 3 4 5   6 7 4 8   9 10 11   L 12 13 14

W 15   L L   L 16 17   5 18 19 20   F 4   M 1   L 5

4 21 14   5 22 19 23   14 24 25 26 27 28 14 4 29 6 30

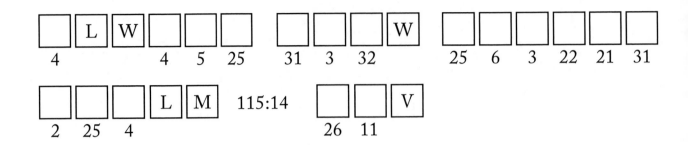

Word List

kind	*stick*	*parents*	*your*
be	*honor*	*together*	

Relationships

Elders

WHAT'S THE POINT?

GOD HAS PLACED PEOPLE IN AUTHORITY OVER OUR LIVES AND WE NEED TO TREAT THEM WITH HONOR AND RESPECT.

theme verse

For all authority comes from God, and those in positions of authority have been placed there by God.

Romans 13:1

related bible story

Jesus on Authority
Matthew 22:15-21

❋ Large Group Lesson ❋

We have talked a lot so far about the relationships that God brings into our lives to help us. We have talked about friends that come along side of us and are our companions on our journey. We have talked about our families who stand by us and help take care of us. But today we are going to talk about one more group of people who God brings into our world to teach us. They are called "elders."

Now, that is kind of a funny old fashioned word that we don't use very much. But let me tell you who your "elders "are. An elder is anyone older than you, anyone who is in leadership over you, or anyone who has any kind of authority in your life. Let's take a closer look at each of those three areas and see who the "elders" are in your life.

First of all, an elder is

→ 1. Someone OLDER than you.

Can you think of someone in your life who is older than you? Yes, your friend down the street may be two months older than you, but that doesn't necessarily make her your elder. What I'm talking about is someone who is a few years older than you or an adult. It could be your parents, grandparents, aunt and uncle, teacher, or simply someone walking on the street that is older than you. Those people are your elders because they were born before you.

We are supposed to honor the people who are older than us. They have experienced lots of things in their lives that you haven't experienced yet, and God wants you to honor them with your words, actions, and attitude. When you honor them, you are recognizing that they know things you don't know and that you respect their position.

Caroline was getting on a bus at the airport to go on vacation with her family. The bus was really crowded and there were only a few more seats available. Caroline had just settled into her seat when a woman who looked about the age of her grandmother walked onto the bus. There were no seats left, and the woman was left standing in the middle of the aisle. As soon as Caroline's Dad noticed the woman standing there, he jumped up and offered his seat to the older woman. She thanked him and quietly slipped into her Father's seat.

After they got off the plane, Caroline asked her Dad a question. "Dad, why did you give that woman your seat on the bus?" "Well," her Dad replied, "it is a way that I honor her because she is older than me. It was something I could do to show her respect."

There are lots of ways that we can honor the older people in our lives. Caroline's Dad showed us a HUGE way – and that is by doing kind things for people older than us. Offering them our seat, opening a door for them, helping them carry something to their car… these are all ways in which we can show respect for someone older than us.

Another way you can honor your elders is by being kind and nice to people who are older. Sometimes younger people don't really appreciate people who are older than them. They can ignore them or sometimes even make fun of them. But that is not at all the kind of attitude God wants you to have toward people older than you. God wants you to honor and respect the elders in your life. Simply because they have gone before you and have wisdom and experiences that you can learn from!

1 Peter 5:5 says, "*In the same way, you younger men must accept the authority of the elders. And all of you, serve each other in humility, for God opposes the proud but favors the humble.*" God wants you to have a humble, serving heart toward the older people in your life. This attitude pleases God and He will bless you for your sweet heart towards your elders.

The second group of people that are your elders are

⇒ **2. Those who are in LEADERSHIP over you.**

Irene was really excited to join the book club her local library was starting. She was so looking forward to spending time with other girls who loved to read as much as she did and discussing all her favorite books.

The first day of book club, she met Stacy, who was the leader of the group. Stacy was only a couple of years older than Irene, but the librarian had put her in charge of the group. Irene instantly knew that Stacy was going to get on her nerves. She was kind of a know-it-all and never really gave the other girls in the group a chance to talk. She was also pretty bossy and set up a whole lot of rules and guidelines as to how the book club was going to run.

Every time Irene would head to the library for book club, she would start to get frustrated. She thought to herself, "I could do a way better job leading the group than Stacy is." She would think negatively about Stacy and her silly rules and super smarty pants attitude.

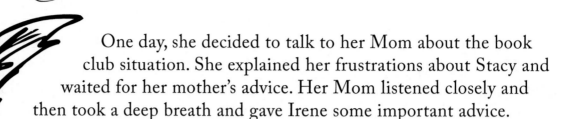

One day, she decided to talk to her Mom about the book club situation. She explained her frustrations about Stacy and waited for her mother's advice. Her Mom listened closely and then took a deep breath and gave Irene some important advice.

"You know honey, I know that sometimes it's difficult to be in a group where the leader does things differently than you would do them. I have been in the same position many times myself. But, as long as you are a part of the group, you need to honor Stacy's leadership. You can do that by keeping a good attitude, trying to follow the rules and guidelines that she has set up, and by keeping your words and actions kind and loving even when you are frustrated."

This wasn't exactly the answer that Irene was hoping for. She wanted her Mom to say that if Stacy was bugging her so much, then she should just quit the group or tell her that she didn't like the way she was doing things. But her Mom was trying to teach her a very important lesson: it's important that we honor people who are in leadership over us even if we don't always like or agree with the way they are leading.

You see, the Bible tells us that ANYONE who is in ANY position of leadership over us has been put there by God. SERIOUSLY! Anyone who is a teacher, leader, mentor, or any other position of leadership in your life has been put there by God because He wants you to learn something from them. Sometimes we can forget that – especially if we're frustrated with our teacher, small group leader, student council president, or anyone else who is your leader.

But God tells us specifically how we should treat people who are in leadership over us. Romans 13:1 tells us, "*Everyone must submit to governing authorities. For all authority comes from God, and those in positions of authority have been placed there by God.*" God has put them in their place, and so our attitude should be respectful.

When you honor the leaders in your life, you are really saying, "God, I trust that you put this person in my life to teach me something." Perhaps God has given you a leader who will show you how to be kind and treat people well. Maybe God has given you a leader that can teach you special knowledge and insight they may have. Or maybe they have a specific skill or talent that they can help you grow or develop.

And sometimes, God allows us to be under a leader who simply shows us the way NOT to do things. No matter what, our response to people in leadership should be one of respect.

Irene decided to be the best book club member she could possibly be, even though it was really hard sometimes. She decided to honor the commitment she made to be in the group and not to quit. She respectfully followed the rules that Stacy set up, and when she made suggestions as to how to make the group better, she did so in a respectful and humble attitude.

When the year ended, the librarian called her up and asked her if SHE would be interested in leading the group for the next year. Hmmmmmmm.... Very interesting!

Do you know what? Irene was very excited to lead the group, and she knew EXACTLY the way she was going to lead the group. She knew that she wanted to give the other girls plenty of time to share their opinions because she knew how frustrating it was when Stacy dominated the conversation. She knew she wanted guidelines, but she approached the rules of the club differently than Stacy did because of her own experience.

Irene realized that God had rewarded her decision to honor the leader that He had put over her. She knew that there were a lot of things that she had learned from Stacy that were really helpful when it came time for HER to lead the group. And she was especially thankful that she had been respectful of Stacy when she was in charge, because this was the kind of attitude she wanted the members of her group to have toward her now. (Remember?!?!? Super-secret special weapon?!? Treat others the way you want to be treated?!??!)

God will put hundreds of people in leadership over you during your lifetime. You can make a decision right now to be respectful, honoring, and someone with a good attitude to all the people in leadership over you.

So, God wants us to honor people older than us, people in leadership over us, and lastly, God wants us to honor

⟹3. People in AUTHORITY over us.

Who is an authority in your life? Basically, it's anyone who has the power to get you into trouble. Your parents are your authority. Your teachers and principals are your authority. Your grandparents and aunts and uncles are your authority. The policemen in your town are your authority. Even the president is an authority over you!

1 Peter 2:13-14 tells us, "*For the Lord's sake, respect all human authority—whether the king as head of state, or the officials he has appointed.*" God puts people in positions of authority in our families, communities, cities, and even our country. They are in the positions they are in because God has placed them there for a specific plan and purpose.

We are supposed to respect those people by honoring them with our attitude, speaking respectfully about them with our words, and by obeying the rules they put over us.

Sometimes we don't agree with everything the people in authority over us think or believe, but God still wants us to respect and honor them. It can be really easy to get frustrated and disappointed in the way some leaders behave, but God tells us that we should pray for them and maintain a respectful attitude even in our disagreement with them.

Jesus actually was caught in a situation where some people were trying to get him to say something bad about the people in authority over him. During the days when Jesus was teaching on the earth, the people in charge of the government were the Romans and they were led by a man named Caesar. Now, they were not leaders who honored God. Actually, they kind of looked at their country as a god. They wanted people to worship them and didn't like it when the people served God.

There were also some religious leaders who didn't like Jesus. They were trying to find ways to get Him in trouble and to make Him look bad in front of other people. So, one day, they asked Him a question in front of the crowds.

Matthew 22:15-21 says, *"Then the Pharisees met together to plot how to trap Jesus into saying something for which he could be arrested. They sent some of their disciples, along with the supporters of Herod, to meet with him. "Teacher," they said, "We know how honest you are. You teach the way of God truthfully. You are impartial and don't play favorites. Now tell us what you think about this: Is it right to pay taxes to Caesar or not?"*

But Jesus knew their evil motives. "You hypocrites!" he said. "Why are you trying to trap me? Here, show me the coin used for the tax." When they handed him a Roman coin, he asked, "Whose picture and title are stamped on it?"

"Caesar's," they replied.

"Well, then," he said, "give to Caesar what belongs to Caesar, and give to God what belongs to God."

His reply amazed them, and they went away."

You see, the religious leaders were hoping to get Jesus to say something bad about the government and people in authority over the area where He was living. But Jesus refused to do it. He chose to honor the authority that God has placed over Him, even though He didn't like A LOT of the things they were saying and doing. He recognized the importance of honoring the authority God had place in leadership at the time.

You can honor those in authority in your life by speaking respectfully about them. You can honor the authority in your life by following the rules and laws of the land. And you can especially honor authority by praying for them and doing everything you can to be a Godly influence and example to all the people you come into contact with.

God wants you to be respectful of your elders. It pleases His heart when you honor those in leadership over you.

You know why? Cause when you respect the elders in your life you are really respecting God. You are acknowledging that He is in charge of everything and that you trust that He is simply putting you right where you need to be. You are trusting His plan for your life. You are saying that you believe that He is in control even if you don't always understand how or why He is doing the things He is doing.

Honor the authority in your life. Sometimes it is hard, but God will help you have the right attitude. He will help you be a good example to others of what it means to live a life that belongs to Jesus.

Closing Prayer: *Dear God. I want to honor you by honoring the elders in my life. Help me to treat the older people in my life with dignity and respect. Show me how I can support and learn from people who You have put in leadership over my life. And I pray for the people in authority in my school, city, and country. I pray that you would give them wisdom and teach me how to have a respectful and helpful attitude toward them. I love you, Jesus, Amen.*

Kindergarten and 1st Grade Group Discussion Questions

1. What is an "elder?"

   a. Someone older than you

   b. Someone in leadership over you

   c. Someone who is an authority in your life

2. Who are some people in your life who are older than you? What are some ways that you can honor and respect them?

3. Who are some of the people in leadership in your life?

   a. Teachers

   b. Parents

   c. Church leaders

   d. Small group leaders

   e. People in charge of clubs you are in

4. What are some ways you can honor the people who are leaders in your life?

   a. By doing what they say

   b. By speaking respectfully to them

   c. By listening while they are talking

   d. By obeying them

   e. By having a good attitude

5. Name some people who are in authority in your life.

   a. Teacher and principals

   b. Parents

   c. Policemen

   d. Government

   e. President

6. The Bible tells us that God gives these people positions of authority. Practice saying the theme verse together. "*For all **authority** comes from God, and those in positions of authority have been placed there by God.*" – Romans 13:1

7. What are some ways you can respect the people in **authority** over you?
   a. Pray for them
   b. Obey the rules and laws
   c. Be kind to them

Polka Dot Talk

2nd and 3rd Grade Group Discussion Questions

1. What is an "elder?"
   a. Someone older than you
   b. Someone in leadership over you
   c. Someone who is an authority in your life

2. Who are some people in your life who are older than you? What are some ways that you can honor and respect them?

3. Who are some of the people in leadership in your life?
   a. Teachers
   b. Parents
   c. Church leaders
   d. Small group leaders
   e. People in charge of clubs you are in

4. Have you ever been in a group when you've been frustrated with the person leading? Share your experience with the group.

5. What are some ways you can honor your leaders, even if you may not love everything about the way they are leading?
   a. Be faithful
   b. Be respectful
   c. Don't talk bad about them to other people
   d. When you offer suggestions, do it with a right attitude.
   e. Pray for them

6. What are some ways you can honor the people who are leaders in your life?
   a. By doing what they say
   b. By speaking respectfully to them
   c. By listening while they are talking
   d. By obeying them
   e. By having a good attitude

7. Name some people who are in authority in your life.
   a. Teacher and principals
   b. Parents
   c. Policemen
   d. Government
   e. President

8. The Bible tells us that God gives these people positions of authority. Practice saying the theme verse together. "*For all **authority** comes from God, and those in positions of **authority** have been placed there by God.*" – Romans 13:1

9. What are some ways you can respect the people in authority over you?
   a. Pray for them
   b. Obey the rules and laws
   c. Be kind to them

4th and 5th Grade
Group Discussion Questions

1. What is an "elder?"
   a. Someone older than you
   b. Someone in leadership over you
   c. Someone who is an authority in your life

2. Who are some people in your life who are older than you? What are some ways that you can honor and respect them?

3. Who are some of the people in leadership in your life?
   a. Teachers
   b. Parents
   c. Church leaders
   d. Small group leaders
   e. People in charge of clubs you are in

4. Have you ever been in a group when you've been frustrated with the person leading? Share your experience with the group.

5. What are some ways you can honor your leaders, even if you may not love everything about the way they are leading?
   a. Be faithful
   b. Be respectful
   c. Don't talk bad about them to other people
   d. When you offer suggestions, do it with a right attitude.
   e. Pray for them

6. What are some ways you can honor the people who are leaders in your life?

   a. By doing what they say

   b. By speaking respectfully to them

   c. By listening while they are talking

   d. By obeying them

   e. By having a good attitude

7. Name some people who are in authority in your life.

   a. Teacher and principals

   b. Parents

   c. Policemen

   d. Government

   e. President

8. The Bible tells us that God gives these people positions of authority. Practice saying the theme verse together. "*For all **authority** comes from God, and those in positions of **authority** have been placed there by God.*" – Romans 13:1

9. What are some ways you can respect the people in authority over you?

   a. Pray for them

   b. Obey the rules and laws

   c. Be kind to them

Candy Bar Award

Supplies Needed:
- 1.55 oz. Hershey Bar/per girl
- Candy Bar Template
- Cardstock in a variety of colors
- Scissors
- Crayons/Markers
- Double stick tape or glue stick
- Embellishments (optional)

Prep:
- Copy template on to cardstock
- Trim excess paper around the template
- Purchase Hershey Bars

What Should We Do Next?
- Color and decorate the candy bar wrapper.
- Write sentiments of thanks and appreciation on the wrapper.
- Wrap the candy bar wrapper around the Hershey Bar.
- Use double stick tape or a glue stick to seal the wrapper at the back of the candy bar.
- You can keep the original wrapper or take it off the bar.
- Give to a grandparent, teacher or leader to show them how much they are appreciated!

CANDY BAR

NET WT 1.55 oz

Nutrition Facts

Serving Size: 1

Good Elder

Romans 13:1 NLT

Amount / Serving	%DV
Appreciation	100%
Honor	100%
Respect	100%
Trust	100%
Happiness	100%

CANDY BAR

NET WT 1.55 oz

Nutrition Facts

Serving Size: 1

Good Elder

Romans 13:1 NLT

Amount / Serving	%DV
Appreciation	100%
Honor	100%
Respect	100%
Trust	100%
Happiness	100%

Polka Dot Plus

Weekly Challenge

Grow – Find out who the leaders in your school and community are. Who is the mayor of your town? Who is the principal of your school? Find out their names and then pray for them!

Love – Write a note to say thank you to someone older than you. Tell them that you appreciate all that they bring to your life!

Act – Find a way to help someone older than you this week. Maybe you can open a door for someone, help them clean up their yard, or carry something for them.

Memorize – Memorize this week's theme verse.

"For all authority comes from God, and those in positions of authority have been placed there by God."

Romans 13:1

Parent Partner

I think many people look at honoring your elders as a sentimental thing that we "used" to do. It's not necessarily fashionable or popular, and so sometimes we can think that it is simply old fashioned to honor your elders.

But the truth is that honoring your elders and people in authority isn't simply something nice, it is a Biblical principle and something that the scripture covers extensively.

Romans 13:1 tells us, *"For all **authority** comes from God, and those in positions of authority have been placed there by God."* Every person who is in leadership and authority over us has been placed there by God. We must teach our children to respect those older than them, those in leadership over them, and those in authority in their lives.

This week, we encouraged the girls to find ways to respect these three groups of people. To honor those who are older than them by having a good attitude, speaking respectfully to them, and assisting them whenever they can. We challenged them to honor those in leadership over them even if they don't always like their leadership. And we taught them to respect the authority in their schools, communities and country by having an attitude of respect and honor and by praying for those who are in positions of authority.

It's pretty common in our society for us to simply haul off and say whatever we think about anyone in politics, leadership, or authority. There is such a lack of respect for people that it can be something our children easily pick up on from TV, media, (ah-hum… and from our mouths too….) Cultivate a healthy attitude as to how you speak about those in leadership over you. You don't have to like the things they do, but God tells us that we must maintain a level of respect simply because we know that God has given them their place of authority and leadership. Your daughter will learn from your example.

Polka Dot Plus

Kindergarten and 1st Grade
Take Home Activity Sheet

God wants you to be respectful of your elders. It pleases His heart when you honor those in leadership over you.

In the heart draw a picture of you and an elder in your life.

What are some ways you can respect the people in authority over you?

Solve each puzzle by substituting the letters for the numbers.

KEY

1	2	3	4	5	6	7	8	9	10	11	12
D	K	A	N	R	E	Y	I	B	P	I	O

1. ____ ____ ____ ____
    10   5   3   7

2. ____ ____ ____ ____
    12   9   6   7

3. ____ ____   ____ ____ ____ ____
    9   6   2   11   4   1

2nd and 3rd Grade
Take Home Activity Sheet

God wants you to be respectful of your elders. It pleases His heart when you honor those in leadership over you.

In the heart draw a picture of you and an elder in your life.

*For all **authority** comes from God, and those in positions of **authority** have been placed there by God.* – Romans 13:1 NLT

What are some ways you can honor the people who are leaders in your life?

Unscramble the words to find your answer.

SCRAMBLED WORDS   WRITE YOUR ANSWERS HERE

1. ISELTN   _____

2. OYEB   _____

3. RPAY   _____

4. EAHV A DGOO TDETUTAI   _____

_____

Answers: Pray, Obey, Listen, Have a good attitude

4th and 5th Grade
Take Home Activity Sheet

Solve the Scripture Puzzle

Step 1: Unscramble each of the clue words to solve the following statement:

An elder is anyone _____ than you, anyone who is in

_____ over you, or anyone who has any kind of

_____ in your life.

CLUE WORDS:

ERDOL   ____   ____   ____   ____   ____

          15   14   22   1   17

RILPEAHESD ____ ____ ____ ____ ____ ____ ____ ____ ____ ____

          23   2   20   24   6   19   8   12   13   21

TORYUHAIT ____ ____ ____ ____ ____ ____ ____ ____ ____

          18   7   9   16   5   3   10   11   4

Answers: Older, Leadership, Authority

Step 2: Copy the letters in the numbered cells above to the cells below with the same number to discover another scripture regarding authority.

___V___ ___ ___ ___N___   M___ ___ ___   ___ ___BM ___ ___
  1   2   3   4   5   6   7   8   9   8   7   10 11

___ ___M ___ ___ ___F   ___ ___   ___ ___ ___
 12 13   8   6   14   9 15   9 16   2

G ___V___ ___N___NG
   5   1   17   10

___ ___ ___ ___ ___ ___ ___ ___ ___ ___ ___ ,   F___ ___
 18   7   9   12   5   19 10   9   13   1   8   5   3

___ ___ ___ ___ ___ ___ ___   ___ ___   N___
 9   12   1   17   1   13   8   5

___ ___ ___ ___ ___ ___ ___ ___ ___   ___XC___ ___ ___
 20   7   9   16   5   3   13   9   4   1   1   21 11

___ ___ ___ ___   W___ ___C___   G___ ___   ___ ___ ___
 9   12 20   9   12   13 12   5   22   12 18   8

___ ___ ___ ___ ___B___ ___ ___ ___ ___ ___   ___ ___ ___
 2   8   9   18   23 10   8   12   1   24   11 12   1

___ ___ ___ ___ ___ ___ ___ ___ ___ ___   ___ ___ ___ ___
 20   7   9   12   5   19 13   9   13   1   8   9   12 18 11

___X___ ___ ___   ___ ___V___   B___ ___N
 2   13   8   9   12 18   1   1   2

___ ___ ___ ___ ___B___ ___ ___ ___ ___ ___   B___   G___ ___.
 1   8   11 20   14 13   8   12   1   24   4   5   24

– Romans 13:1 NIV

Things Change

WHAT'S THE POINT?
EVERYTHING IN THE WORLD CHANGES, BUT GOD WILL NEVER CHANGE.

theme Verse
"I am the Lord, and I do not change."
Malachi 3:6

related bible story
The many changes in the life of Joseph
Genesis 39

❀ Large Group Lesson ❀

What is your favorite season? I LOVE the fall. I love it when the leaves are turning different colors. I love it when the weather starts to turn cooler and you pull out your sweaters and boots. I even like it when the stores are filled with back to school supplies. I may not LOVE the idea that my kids are going back to school – but it sure is fun picking out new pencils and erasers and markers, right? Ok… you don't have to answer that question.

Those first days of school are crazy. Talk about changes! Just a few short weeks before school starts, you are at the pool swimming, sleeping in on summer vacation and staying up late playing with your friends. But every year, no matter how much you try and pretend that it isn't coming, the seasons change, summer ends, and fall begins.

Things change.

Another area that it's really easy to see how things change is in the area of fashion. How many of you have seen pictures of your parents from when they were your age or a teenager. Pretty funny, right?

So – I thought we would take a minute to look at how much things have changed in the area of fashion.

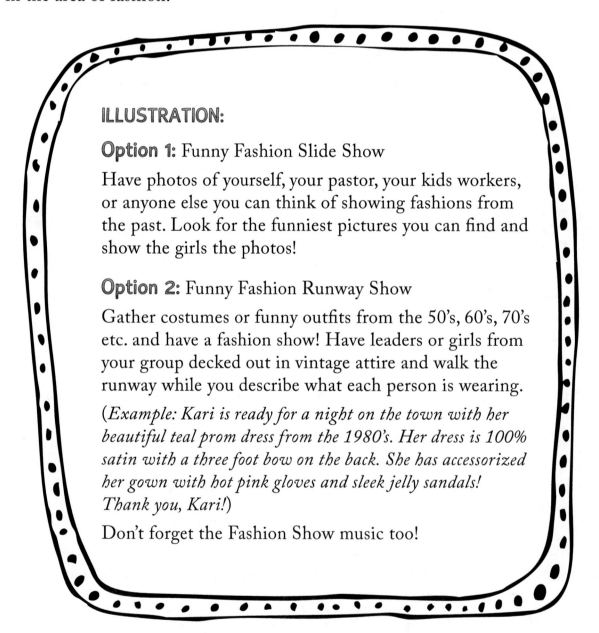

ILLUSTRATION:

Option 1: Funny Fashion Slide Show

Have photos of yourself, your pastor, your kids workers, or anyone else you can think of showing fashions from the past. Look for the funniest pictures you can find and show the girls the photos!

Option 2: Funny Fashion Runway Show

Gather costumes or funny outfits from the 50's, 60's, 70's etc. and have a fashion show! Have leaders or girls from your group decked out in vintage attire and walk the runway while you describe what each person is wearing.

(*Example: Kari is ready for a night on the town with her beautiful teal prom dress from the 1980's. Her dress is 100% satin with a three foot bow on the back. She has accessorized her gown with hot pink gloves and sleek jelly sandals! Thank you, Kari!*)

Don't forget the Fashion Show music too!

Well, I don't know about you, but I'm pretty glad some things change. I'm glad we don't have to wear some of that stuff!

But you know, not all change is fun. Sometimes change can be really hard. There are a lot of things in my life that have changed and sometimes I've had a really hard time adjusting to those changes.

Change is HARD.

Maybe you have had some things change in your life and you've had a hard time working through them. Maybe you have had to change schools and you are struggling to fit in at your new school and you're really missing your old friends.

Maybe your family has changed. Maybe you have a new brother or sister or maybe things have changed between your parents and you've had to adjust to BIG changes at home.

Maybe your friends are changing. Maybe you have had a friend move away. Or maybe the girls that you used to be really close to just aren't that close any more. Maybe they're starting to be interested in things you aren't interested in and you find yourselves just drifting apart.

Maybe you are dealing with a sickness or something with your health that makes you unable to do things like you used to do, and so you have to change the way you spend your time.

Or maybe YOU are changing. You are getting older. You don't feel the same as you used to and you kind of feel like your whole life is upside down.

Change is hard. And change happens to everyone!

Just when you think you have everything figured out, something happens and you have to start all over again!

It can be really frustrating to have to deal with things changing all the time. It can make you feel sad, scared, discouraged, and lots of other things. It can make you feel like you are on shaky ground.

How many of you have ever been in a bouncy house? You know, those big things filled with air where you jump up and down. Or maybe you've been on a trampoline with a bunch of other people. Have you ever tried to walk through a bouncy house or walk on a trampoline when other people are jumping all around you?

You try to steady yourself and walk, but with every step the ground around you lifts and dips and moves. You try to shift your weight to keep your balance, but just when you think you have a steady place to stand, the ground beneath you moves again and you fall on your booty!

Sometimes that is EXACTLY how it feels trying to walk through your life when everything around you is changing. You can feel like you can't quite get your footing. You can feel lost. You can feel shaky and insecure. You might be wondering what you can count on when you look at everything around you that keeps changing.

The truth is: things change. Actually, everything in the whole entire world changes and will continue to change except one thing. Do you know what that is?

GOD.

God never changes. He is always the same. Always. Forever. You can count on it.

No matter how many things in your life are changing – He is always the same.

> *I am the Lord, and I do not change.*
> Malachi 3:6

God will never, ever change. He is exactly the same today as He has always been. That can be hard for us to understand – because everything around us changes. But the truth is that God will remain EXACTLY the same no matter what.

Hebrews 13:8 says, that *"Jesus Christ is the same yesterday, today, and forever."* He will NEVER, EVER change.

And so we can lean on God to help us with whatever changes we are going through!

Now imagine that you are back in that bouncy house with everything moving and shaking when suddenly you see a handle along the edge of the wall. You grab onto it and suddenly, even though everything around you is moving, you are able to keep your balance because you are holding onto the handle.

Or imagine that you are on that bouncy-wouncy trampoline. And suddenly a friend who is standing along the edge reaches out a hand to you. As you walk forward, the ground beneath you is still moving like crazy, but you're not falling because you have something steady to hold onto.

You know what? When you are going through changes in your life and you feel like everything is topsy-turvy, GOD will be like that handle that you can grab onto so you can stay steady. When everything around you feels like it's on shaky ground, GOD will be that hand that reaches out and gives you something strong and stable to keep you from falling.

He will be something that you can keep your eyes on while everything else is going crazy around you. He will be someone that will keep you steady when you don't know who or what you can count on! When everything around you is changing, and you don't know what to do, GOD will remain steady and sure.

So, how do we get through all the changes in our lives? What do we do when things around us are changing and we don't know what to do?

⇒ 1. Remember that change is hard.

Can I tell you something? It's ok to be sad about the things that are changing in your world. It's ok to feel upset that your friend doesn't live here anymore. It's ok to be nervous going to a new school or a new church. It's ok to be upset that your parents are having problems. I think it's really important to be honest about how you're feeling.

Have you ever just been in a really BAD mood? You're just cranky and upset and you don't really know why? Sometimes I get that way and the best thing I know to do in those moments is to just sit down and ask myself, "What am I upset about?"

Once I do that, I usually feel a lot better and can start to deal with whatever situation is bothering me instead of just sitting there being a crabby pants.

I think it's important to admit to yourself that you are having a hard time with the changes in your life. And more important than that – it's so good to come to Jesus and tell him about the things that are bothering you. He already knows – cause He knows everything about you! But when we come to Him and pour out our hearts to Him and ask Him to help us deal with the changes in our lives -something really cool happens.

First of all, He will help us! He will give us creative ideas for dealing with the situation. He will give us patience and peace to face anything that comes our way.

And He will also comfort us! This means that when we are feeling sad or upset, God will help us feel better. He will remind you of how much He loves you and just how very special you are to Him. That sure makes me feel better!

The second way that you and I can deal with change in our lives is to

⇨ 2. Remember that God is with you.

There's a story in the Bible about a guy who went through a WHOLE lot of changes. His name was Joseph.

Joseph had twelve brothers. When he was 17 years old, he told his dad some of the bad things that his brothers were doing and after that they did NOT like him at all! So one day, they threw him into a big pit and then they sold him as a slave to Egypt.

Yikes!! Those were some PRETTY big changes for Joseph! His family fell apart and his brothers SOLD him! He had to go to a new country where He didn't know anyone. Can you imagine how hard that would have been?

But God was with Joseph in every change He went through.

ILLUSTRATION:

Read the story of Joseph found in **Genesis 39** listed below. Have the girls raise their hands every time you say, "*The Lord was with Joseph.*"

Vs 1-4: *When Joseph was taken to Egypt by the Ishmaelite traders; he was purchased by Potiphar, an Egyptian officer. Potiphar was captain of the guard for Pharaoh, the king of Egypt.*

The Lord was with Joseph**, so he succeeded in everything he did as he served in the home of his Egyptian master. Potiphar noticed this and realized that **the Lord was with Joseph.

Then Potiphar's wife made up an awful story about Joseph and told her husband a big lie.

Vs19-23: *Potiphar was furious when he heard his wife's story about how Joseph had treated her. So he took Joseph and threw him into the prison where the king's prisoners were held, and there he remained. But **the Lord was with Joseph** in the prison and showed him his faithful love. And the Lord made Joseph a favorite with the prison warden. Before long, the warden put Joseph in charge of all the other prisoners and over everything that happened in the prison. The warden had no more worries, because Joseph took care of everything. **The Lord was with him** and caused everything he did to succeed.*

Joseph's life was on pretty shaky ground! But no matter what he faced or how crazy things got, God was with Joseph. When he was sad – God was there. When he was scared – God was there. When he was lonely – God was there. When he had no idea what to do – God was there.

And God will be there for you too!

Hebrews 13:5 says, "*Since God assured us, "I'll never let you down, never walk off and leave you."* (MSG)

When YOU are sad – God will be there.
When YOU are scared – God will be there.
When YOU are lonely – God will be there.
When YOU have no idea what to do – God will be there.

Always. Forever. No exceptions. He is not going anywhere. You can be SURE that He will always be with you – no matter what.

And the last way you deal with change in your life is to:

➔ 3. Look ahead.

The hardest thing about change is that you MISS the way things were before! You think back to the way things used to be and you can't imagine things being as good as that ever again.

You wonder if you'll ever have as good of friends as you had before. You wonder if you'll ever feel happy with your family with all the new changes. You wonder if you'll ever like your new school. You wonder if you'll ever feel confident about yourself again.

But – you know what? God has great things AHEAD for you!

You might not be able to see it right now. You might not be able to figure out how it's going to all work out. You might not even feel like it. BUT GOD has great things ahead for you!

1 Peter 1:6 says, "*So be truly glad. There is wonderful joy ahead, even though you have to endure many trials for a little while.*" Things might be hard for a little while when you are dealing with changes, but there is wonderful JOY ahead of you.

The best way to get through a change is to keep your eyes on what is ahead. Philippians 3:13 says, "*Brothers and sisters, I myself don't think I've reached it, but I do this one thing: I forget about the things behind me and reach out for the things ahead of me.*" (CEB)

Now, to forget what is behind – does that mean that we can't still love our old friends? Does it mean we can't remember how great those old times were? Does it mean you can't wish your family would be the way it used to be?

Polka Dot Girls ❀ Relationships

No Way! What is DOES mean is that you can't stop living your life and get STUCK where you are because you won't look ahead to what God has for you. You can remember and love ALL the things that used to be – and still reach out for all the things that God has planned for your future.

God has GREAT things ahead of you! He has new friends for you to meet. He has new things He wants you to do. He has plans to help you deal with your new family situation. He has new things for you to learn. He has new places for you to make a difference. And great big exciting things for every area of your life.

And HE is going to BE THERE for each and every one of them.

James 1:17 says, "*Every good gift, every perfect gift, comes from above. These gifts come down from the Father, the creator of the heavenly lights, in whose character there is no change at all.*" (CEB)

You can look forward to what God has for you because you KNOW that He is going to be there. Hebrews 1:10-11 says, "*Earth and sky will wear out, but not you; they become threadbare like an old coat; You'll fold them up like a worn-out cloak, and lay them away on the shelf. But you'll stay the same, year after year; you'll never fade, you'll never wear out.*" (MSG)

Everything changes. People change. Circumstances change. Families Change. Jobs and schools change.

BUT GOD NEVER, EVER CHANGES.

Closing Prayer: *Dear God, There are a lot of things that are changing in my life. I need you to help me work through these things in my life. Help me to know that you are with me, and to trust that you have great things in store for my future. I love you. Amen.*

Kindergarten and 1st Grade
Group Discussion Questions

1. What are some things that have changed in your life in the last year?

   a. Going to a new school

   b. Going to school all day

   c. Getting a new brother or sister

   d. Moving to a new house

2. Have you ever been in a bouncy house or on a trampoline? What does it feel like to try and walk when everything around you is bouncy?!

   a. It feels crazy!

   b. It's difficult to keep your balance

   c. You fall down.

3. But when you have something or someone to hold onto, it becomes much easier to walk, right? When things are changing in our lives and we feel a little unsteady, who will help us not to fall?

   a. God!

4. Why can God be our steady hand?

   a. Because HE never changes

   b. When everything around us is changing, He will ALWAYS remain the same!

5. Practice saying the theme verse together:
   "I am the Lord, and I do not change." – Malachi 3:6

6. It's important to remember that no matter what changes are going on in your life, that God will always be with you. How does that make you feel when you know God will never leave your side?

   a. Safe

   b. Happy

   c. Not afraid

   d. Not lonely

7. Even though things change all the time, God has NEW things for you! What are some new things that you think God has planned for you?

   a. New friends

   b. New things for you to do

   c. If you moved to a new house, you may have a fun new room in your new house to decorate!

   d. A new brother or sister to help take care of!

   e. A new teacher to get to know

2nd and 3rd Grade
Group Discussion Questions

1. What are some things that have changed in your life in the last year?

   a. Going to a new school

   b. Going to school all day

   c. Getting a new brother or sister

   d. Moving to a new house

   e. Maybe a change in your friendships

   f. School has gotten more difficult

2. Have you ever been in a bouncy house or on a trampoline? What does it feel like to try and walk when everything around you is bouncy?!

   a. It feels crazy!

   b. It's difficult to keep your balance

   c. You fall down.

3. But when you have something or someone to hold onto, it becomes much easier to walk, right? When things are changing in our lives and we feel a little unsteady, who will help us not to fall?

   a. God!

4. Why can God be our steady hand?

   a. Because HE never changes

   b. When everything around us is changing, He will ALWAYS remain the same!

5. Practice saying the theme verse together:
   "I am the Lord, and I do not change." – Malachi 3:6

6. It's important to remember that no matter what changes are going on in your life, that God will always be with you. How does that make you feel when you know God will never leave your side?

    a. Safe

    b. Happy

    c. Not afraid

    d. Not lonely

7. Even though things change all the time, God has NEW things for you! What are some new things that you think God has planned for you?

    a. New friends

    b. New things for you to do

    c. If you moved to a new house, you may have a fun new room in your new house to decorate!

    d. A new brother or sister to help take care of!

    e. A new teacher to get to know

Polka Dot Talk

4th and 5th Grade
Group Discussion Questions

1. What are some things that have changed in your life in the last year?
   a. Going to a new school
   b. Going to school all day
   c. Getting a new brother or sister
   d. Moving to a new house
   e. School has gotten more difficult
   f. *YOU* are changing – you don't like to do things you used to like to do
   g. You aren't friends with the people you used to be friends with

2. Have you ever been in a bouncy house or on a trampoline? What does it feel like to try and walk when everything around you is bouncy?!
   a. It feels crazy!
   b. It's difficult to keep your balance
   c. You fall down.

3. But when you have something or someone to hold onto, it becomes much easier to walk, right? When things are changing in our lives and we feel a little unsteady, who will help us not to fall?
   a. God!

4. Why can God be our steady hand?
   a. Because **HE** never changes
   b. When everything around us is changing, He will **ALWAYS** remain the same!

5. Practice saying the theme verse together:
   "I am the Lord, and I do not change." – Malachi 3:6

6. It's important to remember that no matter what changes are going on in your life, that God will always be with you. How does that make you feel when you know God will never leave your side?

   a. Safe

   b. Happy

   c. Not afraid

   d. Not lonely

   e. Confident walking into new situations

7. Even though things change all the time, God has NEW things for you! What are some new things that you think God has planned for you?

   a. New friends

   b. New things for you to do

   c. If you moved to a new house, you may have a fun new room in your new house to decorate!

   d. A new brother or sister to help take care of!

   e. A new teacher to get to know

   f. You're getting older and God is going to help you take on new responsibilities and activities in your life.

8. It can feel really weird when you start to like things you didn't use to like or when the friends you've had since Kindergarten begin to drift away. But that's all a part of growing up. What are some things you can do to help you navigate the changes of growing up?

   a. Stay close to God

   b. Know that it's ok for your friendships to change over time.

   c. Make new friends and keep the old, too!

   d. Be ok liking the things you like – even if none of your friends like them.

   e. Remember that God will be with you during every change in your life. He will help you!

Option 1: God is our ROCK Booklet

<u>Supplies Needed:</u>
- Cardstock
- Crayons
- Markers
- Foam embellishments, stickers to decorate the cover and enhance each page. (optional)
- Stapler

<u>Prep:</u>
- Copy the cover and booklet pages onto cardstock.

<u>What Should We Do Next?</u>
- Color and decorate the cover and each page according to the season.
- Draw a picture of yourself and your family or friends doing your favorite activity in each season!
- Staple the cover and the four pages to make a booklet

Option 2: God is my ROCK Necklace
(RECOMMENDED FOR 4TH AND 5TH GRADE)

<u>Supplies Needed:</u>
- One small rock per girl
- Plain silver 22 gauge floral wire (approximately 15 inches per girl)
- Scissors
- Pencil
- Needle-nose pliers

- Ribbon, cord or leather thread
- Fine point permanent black marker

Prep:
- With the black marker, write *"Malachi 3:6"* on the rock.
- Cut floral wire into 15" length for each girl.
- Cut ribbon, cord or thread into necklace length for each girl.

What Should We Do Next?
- Place the rock at the center of a 15" long piece of wire.
- Wrap the wire around the rock a few times to secure it.
- Twist together the ends, and then wrap the twist around a pencil to form a loop at the top of the rock.
- Use needle nose pliers to close the loop, and then cut off the excess wire with a scissors.
- To finish, thread a necklace length piece of ribbon, cord or leather through the loop and knot the end.

Seasons Change, but GOD does NOT!

By: _____

Spring

"I am the Lord, and I do not change." – Malachi 3:6 NLT

"I am the Lord, and I do not change." – Malachi 3:6 NLT

Fall

"I am the Lord, and I do not change." – Malachi 3:6 NLT

Winter

Summer

"I am the Lord, and I do not change." – Malachi 3:6 NLT

Polka Dot Plus

Weekly Challenge

Grow – Grow closer to God as you talk to Him about how you feel about the changes in your life.

Love – Maybe you have a friend who has had a big change happen in her life. Do something special to remind her that God is with her. Write her a note, draw her a picture, or maybe just give her a hug!

Act – Make a list of some of the things that have changed in your life. Then, make a list of some of the new things that God has in front of you.

Memorize – Memorize this week's theme verse.

"I am the Lord, and I do not change."
Malachi 3:6

Parent Partner

Change is hard for all of us. And for kids, many times they aren't sure how to deal with the things changing around them. They might feel sad or angry or confused or simply resistant to things in their lives that are not the same as they used to be.

Today our Polka Dot Girls lesson focused on the fact that everything in the world will change except God. He will never, ever change. In a world that keeps us re-adjusting, re-adapting, and re-working, there is great comfort in knowing that God will always remain the same. We encouraged them to talk to God about the things that are bothering them. We taught them that God will be with them no matter how big or small the changes in their lives.

And we showed them that, although change is difficult, God has GREAT things in store for them in the future. We encouraged them to look ahead to the new opportunities, friendships, and circumstances that God has planned for them.

Change is hard. But God is big and can help each and every one of us (and our kids, too!) to get through seasons of change with hearts filled with anticipation for what lies ahead.

Polka Dot Plus

Kindergarten and 1st Grade Activity Sheet

Instructions: Finish the rest of the butterfly with your best doodles, then color the caterpillar and butterfly!

I CHANGE, BUT GOD DOES NOT!

Fill in the blanks with either the word CHANGE or SAME. All scripture NIV

"I the LORD do not _____." – Malachi 3:6

"Jesus Christ is the _____ yesterday and today and forever."
– Hebrews 13:8

"But you remain the _____, and your years will never end."
– Psalm 102:27

*"Every good and perfect gift is from above, coming down from the Father of the
heavenly lights, who does not _____ like shifting shadows."*
– James 1:17

Polka Dot Plus

2nd and 3rd Grade
Activity Sheet

Instructions: Finish the rest of the butterfly with your best doodles, then color the caterpillar and butterfly!

I CHANGE, BUT GOD DOES NOT!

Look up the following verses in your Bible and fill in the blanks. All scripture NIV.

"*I the LORD do not _____.*" – Malachi 3:6

"*Jesus Christ is the _____ yesterday and today and forever.*"
– Hebrews 13:8

"*But you remain the _____, and your years will never end.*"
– Psalm 102:27

"*Every good and perfect gift is from above, coming down from the Father of the heavenly lights, who does not _____ like shifting shadows.*"
– James 1:17

"*Brothers, I do not consider myself yet to have taken hold of it. But one thing I do: Forgetting what is _____ and straining toward what is _____,*" – Philippians 3:13

He also says, "In the beginning, O Lord, you laid the foundations of the earth, and the heavens are the work of your _____. They will perish, but you _____; they will all wear out like a garment." – Hebrews 1:10-11

WORD LIST

change	*hands*	*same*	*same*
change	*ahead*	*behind*	*remain*

week 5

4th and 5th Grade Activity Sheet

List 5 things that have changed in your life over the last year.

1.

2.

3.

4.

5.

List 5 new things God has ahead for you.

1.

2.

3.

4.

5.

Look up the following verses in your Bible and fill in the blanks. All scripture NIV.

"I the LORD do not _____." – Malachi 3:6

"Jesus Christ is the _____ yesterday and today and forever."
– Hebrews 13:8

"But you remain the _____, and your years will never end."
– Psalm 102:27

"*Every good and perfect gift is from above, coming down from the Father of the heavenly lights, who does not* _____ *like shifting shadows.*"
– James 1:17

"*Brothers, I do not consider myself yet to have taken hold of it. But one thing I do: Forgetting what is* _____ *and straining toward what is*

_____," – Philippians 3:13

"*In this you greatly* _____, *though now for a little while you may have had to suffer grief in all kinds of trials.*" – 1 Peter 1:6

"*Keep your lives free from the love of money and be* _____ *with what you have, because God has said, "Never will I* _____ *you; never will I* _____ *you.*" – Hebrews 13:5

Word List

change	*rejoice*	*content*	*same*
leave	*change*	*forsake*	*behind*
same	*ahead*		

Relationships

Watch Your Words

What's the Point?

God wants us to choose to use kind and encouraging words.

theme verse

"Words kill, words give life;
they're either poison or fruit—you choose."
Proverbs 18:21 MSG

related bible story

Taming the Tongue
James 3:5-12

❧ Large Group Lesson ❧

Have you ever had someone say something really, really nice about you? Maybe your Mom told everyone in your family something really special about you. Or maybe a teacher pointed out how much she appreciated your help in class. Or maybe a friend thanked you for being in her life.

There is nothing quite as awesome as someone saying something nice to you. Something inside of you just feels SO good when someone speaks kind words to you. You feel happy, confident and proud of yourself. I love it when people say nice things about me!!!

Now, let me ask you THIS question. Have you ever had someone say something "not so nice" about you? Yup… me too. Maybe a friend got mad at you and said some things about you behind your back. Or maybe a teacher said something that hurt your feelings. Or maybe your brother or sister called you a name.

There is nothing quite as AWFUL as having someone say something bad about you. You get a horrible feeling in your stomach and you just want to crawl into bed and cry. You feel sad, nervous, and alone. I HATE it when people say bad things about me!

Isn't it crazy to see how POWERFUL our words are? A kind word from someone can make you feel AMAZING and an unkind word can make you feel HORRIBLE. I think it is amazing how something as little as a WORD can have so much power over how we feel.

The Bible says that "*Words kill, words give life; they're either poison or fruit—you choose.*" (Proverbs 18:21 MSG) What do you think that means? It means that our words have the power to tear people down or build people up. And you and I have to choose what kind of words we are going to use.

Sarah hated going to the bus stop. Every morning she would get on her coat and shoes and backpack and head for the front door and stop and say a prayer because she was SO nervous to walk outside to wait for the bus with the other kids.

The reason WHY she was so nervous was because there were three girls at the bus stop who didn't say very nice things to her. Every morning, they would comment on what she was wearing and whisper and giggle at her. Sarah had NO idea why these girls were so mean to her, but it seemed like no matter what she did, they found something bad to say about her.

Their words were powerful. Even if Sarah got dressed and looked at her outfit and absolutely LOVED it, once the girls at the bus stop finished with her, she always felt horrible about what she was wearing. Their words hurt.

The Bible tells us that our words have the power to hurt, but they also have the power to build someone up. Our words can tear down, but our words also have the power to make us feel stronger and more confident!

One day Sarah got to the bus stop and was bracing herself for the girls to start talking about her. But before they could open their mouths, suddenly another girl spoke up. "Sarah, I love your new coat! I think it is really cool. Where did you get it?" Sarah was shocked! She replied quietly, "Uhm… my Grandma sent it to me." The other girl spoke again. "Well, I think it is the cutest thing I've ever seen… but you always wear the cutest clothes."

Sarah could not believe it. She looked at the mean girls and their mouths were wide open and they simply turned away in a huff. The nice things that this girl said to her quieted the rude comments of the other girls. The power of those nice words was WAY stronger than the power of the negative ones. She was so thankful that this new friend has chosen to use the power of kind words instead of the power of unkind words.

I know that sometimes it can be hard to control the words that are coming from your mouth. There are times that I say things and then I wonder "Why in the world did I say that?!?" It can be easy to say mean things to someone when you are frustrated with them. It can make you feel strong when you use the power of your words to tear someone else down. And you can feel important when you talk about another person.

But God is very clear in the Bible that He wants us to be very, very careful about the words we use. James 3:2 says, *"For if we could control our tongues, we would be perfect and could also control ourselves in every other way."* God knows that if we control our tongues – or if we control the things we say - that we will be able to control ourselves in lots of different areas. Our words may be hard to control, but if we learn to be careful about the things we are saying, we will be able to control LOTS of other things in our hearts!

Here are three ways we can choose to use the power of our words for GOOD and not EVIL.

➡ 1. Don't gossip.

Gossip is simply talking about other people behind their backs. It is sharing information or stories with other people. Most of the time, it's sharing things that are mean and hurtful, but it's even wrong to simply share information that isn't yours to share! Gossip is telling a story that can damage a person's reputation. It is talking or writing about another person or situation in order to turn another's opinion against that person or situation.

Sometimes we gossip because we are upset with a person and we don't know what to do about it. But the Bible tells us that if we have a problem with someone, we shouldn't talk to other people about it – we should go right to the person and talk it through with them! Matthew 18:15 says, "*If a fellow believer hurts you, GO and tell him – work it out between the two of you.*"

Other times we gossip just because it seems fun. Sometimes we can talk about other people simply because we don't have anything better to talk about. Some people just think it's fun to say things about people's clothes or families or lots of other things. We can tell our friends a story that we may think is funny, but really we are just making fun of someone else.

But God does NOT want us to use other people that way. He cares about each and every person and when we say things about other people, it makes God's heart so sad. We should want to honor God by treating other people the way that God would want us to treat them. Psalm 19:14 says, "*Let the words of my mouth and the thoughts of my heart be pleasing to you O Lord.*"

God wants you to be a good friend. When we talk about other people behind their backs, we are not being a good friend.

Another way we can choose positive words is

⇨ 2. Be a trustworthy friend.

I had a friend who liked to talk about other people. She loved to tell what so-and-so did last weekend and who is fighting with whom. She loved to go through all the people we knew and point out all the things about them that she didn't like. She just LOVED to talk about other people.

I never felt comfortable when she talked about other people that way. But one day, something occurred to me that made me really re-think my friendship with her. I began to wonder – if she talked about OTHER PEOPLE all the time behind their backs, chances are she was talking about ME behind my back.

But I have ANOTHER friend, who NEVER talks about other people. And anytime we are with other people and they start to say something about someone else, she either says something positive about that person or changes the subject. I really began to notice how hard she worked at not saying unkind things about people.

That friend made me realize two things. First of all, that I should be a lot more like her!! And secondly, I realized that I could always trust her. I never had to wonder if she was saying bad things about me to other people. I could tell her anything and know that she wouldn't share it with anyone else.

I realized that the way this friend acted made me TRUST her. When you trust someone, it means that you feel safe with them. You don't wonder if they are REALLY your friend or not. You don't have to worry about them behaving one way when they are with you and another way when you're not around.

Not only should you try to fill your life with friends you can trust, you should BECOME a trustworthy friend! Make sure your friends know that they can count on you to only use kind words about them. Show them your loyalty by refusing to talk about ANYONE behind their back. Proverbs 20:19 says, *"A gossip tells secrets, so don't hang around with someone who talks too much."*

The last way we can be a friend who chooses positive words, is to

➡ 3. Encourage other people.

We have talked about how powerful our words are. They can build people up, or they can tear them down. We can choose to use kind words or we can choose to use unkind words.

When you say kind words to people, you are encouraging them! When you point out the good things in people, and tell them what you like about them, you are encouraging them! When you help people feel better about themselves, you are an encourager!

ILLUSTRATION: Love Bucket

<u>What you will need:</u>

• A bucket of some sort (a transparent bucket would be best)

• A number of things to fill the bucket (large heart foam cutouts, balls, jelly beans, whatever you can find!)

Each of us has a love bucket! We want to feel encouraged and loved. When someone uses KIND words toward you, they are filling up your love bucket one little thing at a time. So maybe your friend tells you that she likes your sweater… she is filling your love bucket! (*As you say this, place the object inside the bucket.*) When your teacher tells you that you did a good job… filling the love bucket. (*Continue with examples – even ask the girls some ideas as to how you can fill the love bucket.*)

BUT – when someone uses UNKIND words, they are actually taking things out of your love bucket! Let's say someone tells you that they don't like your new haircut… they are emptying your love bucket (*as you say this, remove an object from the bucket.*) When you and your friend get in a fight and she says something mean to you… they are emptying your love bucket.

So – do you think we should be friends who are emptying out love buckets or filling up love buckets? That's right! We should always find ways to ENCOURAGE and fill up the buckets of the people in our lives.

week 6

Ephesians 4:29 tell us, *"Let everything you say be good and helpful, so that your words will be an encouragement to those who hear them."* Make a decision to be the kind of friend who always says good and helpful things. Be an encouraging friend.

Our words are powerful. We can choose to use our words to encourage and lift up our friends, or we can choose to use our words to tear them down. Let's be the kind of friends who make the right choice!

Closing Prayer: *Dear God, I thank you for the friends and family you have given me. Help me to not use words that tear down other people. Help me to not talk about people behind their backs. I want to be a trustworthy and encouraging friend. I love you, Jesus. Amen.*

Kindergarten and 1st Grade Group Discussion Questions

1. Have you ever had someone say something really nice to you? Share with the group!

2. How did it make you feel when that person said something kind to you?

3. Has someone ever said something unkind to you? How did that make you feel?

4. The Bible tells us that our words are powerful, and we have a choice as to whether we are going to use kind or unkind words. Let's practice saying this week's theme verse together a few times: *"Words kill, words give life; they're either poison or fruit—you choose."* – Proverbs 18:21 MSG

5. What does that verse mean?

   a. Our words can hurt people or our words can help them.

   b. Our words can be poison that hurts someone or our words can be the fruit that fills people up and makes them healthy.

6. What does it mean to gossip?

   a. Talk about people behind their back

   b. To say things about people that aren't true

   c. To tell stories about people that may be true – but make them look bad to other people.

7. What does God say about gossip?

   a. He doesn't want us to gossip

   b. We shouldn't say bad things about other people.

8. What are some ways that you can be a trustworthy friend?

    a. Not talk about anyone so that my friends will know that I won't talk about them when they're not around.

    b. Always build up other people

    c. Be a friend who uses kind words

    d. Be a friend who doesn't share private things with other people.

9. God wants us to be encouraging and fill up people's love buckets! What are some things you can do this week to fill up your friends' love buckets?

    a. Compliment them

    b. Say nice things to them

    c. Tell them they're doing a good job

    d. Encourage them to try something new because you believe in them.

2nd and 3rd Grade
Group Discussion Questions

1. Have you ever had someone say something really nice to you? Share with the group!

2. How did it make you feel when that person said something kind to you?

3. Has someone ever said something unkind to you? How did that make you feel?

4. The Bible tells us that our words are powerful, and we have a choice as to whether we are going to use kind or unkind words. Let's practice saying this week's theme verse together a few times: *"Words kill, words give life; they're either poison or fruit—you choose."* – Proverbs 18:21 MSG

5. What does that verse mean?

   a. Our words can hurt people or our words can help them.

   b. Our words can be poison that hurts someone or our words can be the fruit that fills people up and makes them healthy.

6. What does it mean to gossip?

   a. Talk about people behind their back

   b. To say things about people that aren't true

   c. To tell stories about people that may be true – but make them look bad to other people.

7. What does God say about gossip?

   a. He doesn't want us to gossip

   b. We shouldn't say bad things about other people.

8. What are some ways that you can be a trustworthy friend?

   a. Not talk about anyone so that my friends will know that I won't talk about them when they're not around.

   b. Always build up other people

   c. Be a friend who uses kind words

   d. Be a friend who doesn't share private things with other people.

9. God wants us to be encouraging and fill up people's love buckets! What are some things you can do this week to fill up your friends' love buckets?

   a. Compliment them

   b. Say nice things to them

   c. Tell them they're doing a good job

   d. Encourage them to try something new because you believe in them.

4th and 5th Grade
Group Discussion Questions

1. Have you ever had someone say something really nice to you? Share with the group!

2. How did it make you feel when that person said something kind to you?

3. Has someone ever said something unkind to you? How did that make you feel?

4. The Bible tells us that our words are powerful, and we have a choice as to whether we are going to use kind or unkind words. Let's practice saying this week's theme verse together a few times: *"Words kill, words give life; they're either poison or fruit—you choose."* – Proverbs 18:21 MSG

5. What does that verse mean?

   a. Our words can hurt people or our words can help them.

   b. Our words can be poison that hurts someone or our words can be the fruit that fills people up and makes them healthy.

6. What does it mean to gossip?

   a. Talk about people behind their back

   b. To say things about people that aren't true

   c. To tell stories about people that may be true – but make them look bad to other people.

7. What does God say about gossip?

   a. He doesn't want us to gossip

   b. We shouldn't say bad things about other people.

8. What are some ways that you can be a trustworthy friend?

    a. Not talk about anyone so that my friends will know that I won't talk about them when they're not around.

    b. Always build up other people

    c. Be a friend who uses kind words

    d. Be a friend who doesn't share private things with other people.

9. God wants us to be encouraging and fill up people's love buckets! What are some things you can do this week to fill up your friends' love buckets?

    a. Compliment them

    b. Say nice things to them

    c. Tell them they're doing a good job

    d. Encourage them to try something new because you believe in them.

"Love Bucket" Encouragement Jar

Supplies Needed:

- Ball® 8oz. Regular Mouth Jars with Lids
- Large Clear Plastic Cups (less expensive alternative)
- Encouragement Jar Template
- Avery 5163 labels
- Decorative Stickers
- Ribbon or Raffia
- Scissors or paper cutter
- Colored Cardstock (one piece per girl)
- Foam Hearts (optional)

Prep:

- Print Encouragement Jar template onto Avery 5163 labels
- Cut colored cardstock into ten 2"x 4" size slips of paper.

What Should We Do Next?

- Stick label on the front of the jar.
- Decorate the jar with fun stickers.
- On colored cardstock slips write out encouraging phrases and words such as "You can do it", "I believe in you", "I love you", "You are amazing!" "God loves you", etc.
- For younger girls, draw pictures of a heart, cross, smiley face or anything that would encourage someone.
- After you write out your words and phrases on the slips, place them in the jar.
- Tie a cute bow with ribbon or raffia around the rim of the jar.
- Give to a friend or family member!

Encouragement Jar

Let everything you say be good and helpful,
so that your words will be an encouragement
to those who hear them. – Ephesians 4:29

Encouragement Jar

Let everything you say be good and helpful,
so that your words will be an encouragement
to those who hear them. – Ephesians 4:29

Encouragement Jar

Let everything you say be good and helpful,
so that your words will be an encouragement
to those who hear them. – Ephesians 4:29

Encouragement Jar

Let everything you say be good and helpful,
so that your words will be an encouragement
to those who hear them. – Ephesians 4:29

Encouragement Jar

Let everything you say be good and helpful,
so that your words will be an encouragement
to those who hear them. – Ephesians 4:29

Encouragement Jar

Let everything you say be good and helpful,
so that your words will be an encouragement
to those who hear them. – Ephesians 4:29

Encouragement Jar

Let everything you say be good and helpful,
so that your words will be an encouragement
to those who hear them. – Ephesians 4:29

Encouragement Jar

Let everything you say be good and helpful,
so that your words will be an encouragement
to those who hear them. – Ephesians 4:29

Encouragement Jar

Let everything you say be good and helpful,
so that your words will be an encouragement
to those who hear them. – Ephesians 4:29

Encouragement Jar

Let everything you say be good and helpful,
so that your words will be an encouragement
to those who hear them. – Ephesians 4:29

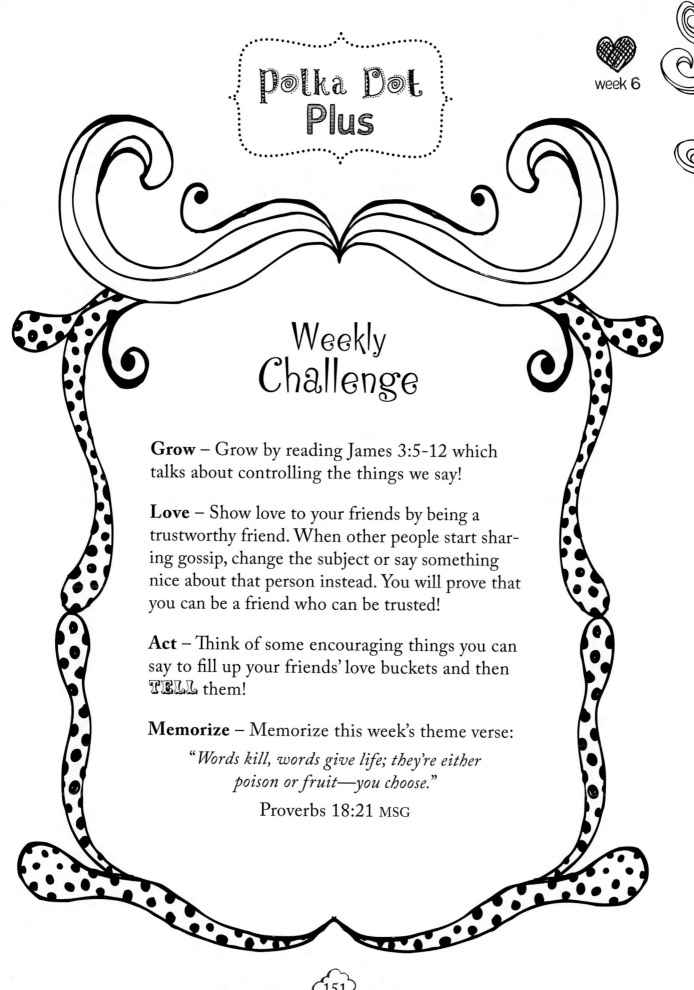

Polka Dot Plus

Weekly Challenge

Grow – Grow by reading James 3:5-12 which talks about controlling the things we say!

Love – Show love to your friends by being a trustworthy friend. When other people start sharing gossip, change the subject or say something nice about that person instead. You will prove that you can be a friend who can be trusted!

Act – Think of some encouraging things you can say to fill up your friends' love buckets and then TELL them!

Memorize – Memorize this week's theme verse:

"Words kill, words give life; they're either poison or fruit—you choose."

Proverbs 18:21 MSG

Parent Partner

This week we talked to our **Polka Dot Girls** about the power of our words. Kind words can encourage us, build us up, and make us feel good about ourselves. And unkind words have the power to discourage us, tear us down, and make us want to crawl under a rock and hide!

We all have a choice as to whether or not we are going to use our powerful words to build up or tear down. Proverbs 18:21 tells us. *"Words kill, words give life; they're either poison or fruit—you choose."* God wants us to choose to speak life into each other by the kind of words we use.

We talked to the girls about gossip and how important it is to not talk about other people behind their backs. We shared the importance of being a trustworthy friend. Our friends should be able to count on the fact that we wouldn't talk badly about them to other people.

And lastly, we inspired them to be encouragers! They have the power of their words; why not use them to help other people feel the best about themselves that they can!

Be a great example to your daughter by carefully choosing the words you use to not only speak to her, but be cautious about how you speak about others in her presence! She will follow your example. If you demonstrate being a trustworthy friend who does not speak ill of people, you will set an extraordinary standard for her as to how she should treat the people she cares about.

Kindergarten and 1st Grade
Take Home Activity Sheet

Each word or phrase has the power to encourage others or hurt others.

Color the encouraging words and draw a line through the words that hurt.

"Words kill, words give life; they're either poison or fruit—you choose."
– Proverbs 18:21 MSG

WAY TO GO!

YOU ARE AWESOME

I DON'T LIKE YOU

I LOVE YOU

YOU CAN DO IT!

THAT'S STUPID

I BELIEVE IN YOU

YOU CAN'T PLAY WITH ME

THANK YOU FOR BEING MY FRIEND

YOU ARE SO GOOD AT THAT!

YOU ARE SO MEAN

I DON'T CARE WHAT YOU SAY

YOU DON'T FIT IN OUR GROUP

God wants us to choose to use kind and encouraging words.

The verses below talk about how we should watch our words. Read each verse in your Bible and draw a picture of the missing word. All scripture NIV

1. James 3:2

We all stumble in many ways. If anyone is never at fault in what he says, he is a

perfect man, able to keep his whole _____ *in check.*

2. Psalm 19:14

May the words of my mouth and the meditation of my _____

be pleasing in your sight, O LORD, my Rock and

my Redeemer.

3. Ephesians 4:29

Do not let any unwholesome talk come out of your _____,

but only what is helpful for building others

up according to their needs, that it may benefit

those who _____.

WORD LIST
heart

body

listen

mouths

Polka Dot Plus

2nd and 3rd Grade
Take Home Activity Sheet

God is very clear in the Bible that He wants us to be very, very careful about the words we use. Your words can build up those around you or tear them down.

Fill in the blanks below to start building up the friends and family in your life.

I can build up _____ with this word of encouragement:

I can build up _____ with this compliment:

I can build up _____ by thanking them for:

I can build up _____ by telling them this about God:

God wants us to choose to use kind and encouraging words.

The verses below talk about how we should watch our words. Read each verse in your Bible and fill in the missing word. All scripture NIV

1. James 3:2

We all stumble in many ways. If anyone is never at fault in what he says, he is a perfect man, able to keep his whole _____ in check.

2. Psalm 19:14

May the words of my mouth and the meditation of my _____ be pleasing in your sight, O LORD, my Rock and my Redeemer.

3. Ephesians 4:29

Do not let any unwholesome talk come out of your _____, but only what is helpful for building others up according to their needs, that it may benefit those who _____.

4. Proverbs 20:19

A _____ betrays a confidence; so avoid a man who talks too much.

5. Matthew 18:15

If your brother _____ against you, go and show him his fault, just between the _____ of you. If he listens to you, you have won your brother over.

Word List

| heart | two | body | listen |
| gossip | sins | mouths | |

Polka Dot Plus

4th and 5th Grade
Take Home Activity Sheet

Each of us has a love bucket! We want to feel encouraged and loved. When someone uses KIND words toward you, they are filling up your love bucket one little thing at a time.

BUT – when someone uses UNKIND words, they are actually taking things out of your love bucket!

One week challenge! Reflect on the following questions and at the end of each day, circle your answers and at the end of the week fill in the blank.

1. Did I fill someone's love bucket this week by being encouraging, kind, helpful or thoughtful?

Monday	Yes	No
Tuesday	Yes	No
Wednesday	Yes	No
Thursday	Yes	No
Friday	Yes	No
Saturday	Yes	No
Sunday	Yes	No

If yes, how? _____

_____

_____

2. Did I say or do anything that might have emptied someone's love bucket, or did I empty someone's bucket by not doing something that I was supposed to do?

Monday   Yes   No

Tuesday   Yes   No

Wednesday   Yes   No

Thursday   Yes   No

Friday   Yes   No

Saturday   Yes   No

Sunday   Yes   No

If yes, how? _____

_____

_____

Did I apologize?   Yes   No

3. Is there anyone I know whose love bucket is less than full and could really use a friend? Yes or No

If yes, how? _____

_____

_____

If yes, what could I do to help? _____

_____

_____

The verses below talk about how we should watch our words. Read each verse in your Bible and fill in the missing word. All scripture NIV

1. James 3:2

"We all stumble in many ways. If anyone is never at fault in what he says, he is a perfect man, able to keep his whole _____ in check."

2. Psalm 19:14

"May the words of my mouth and the meditation of my _____ be pleasing in your sight, O LORD, my Rock and my Redeemer."

3. Ephesians 4:29

"Do not let any unwholesome talk come out of your _____, but only what is helpful for building others up according to their needs, that it may benefit those who _____."

4. Proverbs 20:19

"A _____ betrays a confidence; so avoid a man who talks too much."

5. Matthew 18:15

"If your brother _____ against you, go and show him his fault, just between the _____ of you. If he listens to you, you have won your brother over."

WORD LIST

heart	two	body	listen
gossip	sins	mouths	

Attention

WHAT'S THE POINT?

WE SHOULD BE KNOWN FOR THE GOOD THINGS WE DO — AND NOT TRY TO GET ATTENTION FROM THE THINGS WE WEAR, TRYING TO BE THE CENTER OF ATTENTION, OR DOING NEGATIVE THINGS.

theme verse

For women who claim to be devoted to God should make themselves attractive by the good things they do.
I Timothy 2:10

related bible story

Tabitha
Acts 9:36-43

❀ Large Group Lesson ❀

I L-O-V-E birthdays. I love everything about them. I love all the presents. I love the cake and candles. But mostly, it sure is fun to have a day where everyone points out how special you are. It's so nice to have people say nice things to you and give you gifts. It's fun to have a day where you are the center of attention.

Can you imagine if everyday was your birthday?! If every-where you went, everyday, people stopped you and handed you a gift! Or after every meal, your mom brought out a cake and everyone sang to you?! That would be crazy.... CRAZY AWESOME!

Birthdays are fun because it's always nice to get attention. It feels good when people notice you and tell you that you are special to them. I think for most of us, one of the things most important to us is to feel like we matter to the people around us. We want to know that people love us and care about us. And on our birthdays, people take extra time to make sure we KNOW how important we are to them. It's really, really, nice!

But, what about all those other days? There are 364 days every year that are NOT your birthday. What do we do on those days when we aren't getting special at-tention? Some of you don't really like attention, so you are just fine on the non-birthday days! But for most of us, sometimes we can need more attention than we are getting from those plain everyday days.

Why does attention feel so good? Because we all want to know that we are valu-able. We want to know that we are important to people. We want to feel loved and pretty and liked. When someone gives you attention by saying something nice to you, it makes your heart happy and you feel good about yourself. When someone gives you attention by asking you to spend time with them, you feel im-portant. When someone tells you that you are beautiful, you feel beautiful!

There is nothing wrong with getting attention from other people. Actually, God loves it when we feel good about ourselves because He LOVES us. HE is your #1 fan. He loves every single tiny thing about you. So, when other people value you, He likes it too!

But sometimes, we can get the WRONG kind of attention. People can notice us because of the negative things we do. We can behave in a way that isn't kind and loving and other people notice us for the wrong reason.

There was a girl in Kathy's class that always seemed to have the teacher's attention, but Kathy wasn't so sure that it was the "good kind" of attention. This girl was always getting in trouble for being disrespectful. She would be speak out of turn and say inappropriate things. The teacher spent a lot of time dealing with this girl's behavior. She sure was getting a lot of attention, but it wasn't for positive things.

And sometimes we can get attention by doing or saying things that aren't very honoring to God. Sometimes we can wear clothes that are a little too sassy and people can notice us in a "not so good" kind of way. God doesn't like it when we get that kind of attention. Sometimes we can get attention by telling a joke that has a bad word in it or saying mean things about other people. God doesn't want us to get attention like that either.

Here are three things to remember when it comes to attention.

➡ 1. Don't steal all the attention.

Candace had a friend that REALLY loved to get attention. She loved to talk about the things SHE was doing and point out the new outfit SHE was wearing and make sure everyone knew what SHE wanted to do. She was super nice and really fun to be around, but it seemed like she always had to be the center of attention. After a while, her friends got tired of everything ALWAYS being about her. They got frustrated because she never seemed interested in listening to what THEY had to say. If the conversation wasn't focused on the things that she wanted to talk about, then she simply would stop listening.

God doesn't want us stealing all the attention! He doesn't want us to always make things about ourselves. ACTUALLY, the Bible says, "*Don't be selfish; don't try to impress others. Be humble, thinking of others as better than yourselves.*" (Philippians 2:3). When we are constantly demanding all the attention, we are really being selfish. We are not thinking of other people's feelings; we are simply focusing on ourselves and what we want.

Good friends are interested in what other people have to say. Good friends love to point out the wonderful things in other people. Good friends don't steal all the attention.

Secondly, we need to remember:

➡ 2. Don't try to get attention in negative ways.

It certainly is nice to have people pay attention to you, but sometimes we can start to want it so bad that we're willing to do anything to make people notice us. One way we can do that is by misbehaving just to get someone's attention. We can act out in school, disobey our parents at home, and even fight with our friends. We may be getting attention all right, but it's not for good things!

And sometimes we can try and get attention by doing or saying things that we know we shouldn't say or do. We can put on clothes that make people notice us, but they make us look a way that isn't pleasing to God. The Bible talks about not drawing attention to ourselves by wearing things that make people notice us in a negative way. I Timothy 2:9 says, "*And I want women to be modest in their appearance. They should wear decent and appropriate clothing and not draw attention to themselves by the way they fix their hair or by wearing gold or pearls or expensive clothes.*" Now, does this mean that you can't wear cute clothes or fun jewelry?! NO!

What this scripture is saying is that we need to dress in clothes that cover up our bodies in a way that doesn't look too sassy. Sometimes we can see clothes that are really, really short or have things about them that seem really grown up. We want to make sure that the clothes we wear don't draw so much attention to us that people only notice what we are wearing, and not what's on the inside!

Don't try to get attention from things that aren't good. You are such an amazing and beautiful girl; you don't need all that stuff to make people notice you! You just be the bright shining light that God made you to be – and people will notice you for that!

And the last thing we need to remember is:

⇒ 3. Be known for the good things you do for other people.

There is a story in the Bible about a woman who was known for all the amazing, kind, and generous things she did. Her name was Tabitha. (She is also called Dorcus sometimes. I'm not sure I would like to be called Dorcus… would you?!?) Acts 9:36 says, *"There was a believer in Joppa named Tabitha (which in Greek is Dorcas). She was always doing kind things for others and helping the poor."* One day she became very sick and died. A man named Peter, who was one of Jesus' disciples, was called to the house where she lived.

"So Peter returned with them; and as soon as he arrived, they took him to the upstairs room. The room was filled with widows who were weeping and showing him the coats and other clothes Dorcas had made for them." (Acts 9:39) The house was full of people who knew and loved Tabitha because of the kind things she had done for them. It says that she had made them coats and sewed clothes for them. These were women whose husband's had died and were probably very, very poor. Tabitha had taken it upon herself to take care of them, and that was what she was known for! (PS… you should read the rest of the story in Acts Chapter 9… because something totally incredible happens to Tabitha!!!)

POLKA DOT POINTERS

The name Tabitha is a Hebrew name. Other times in the Bible, they call her by the name Dorcas, which is a Greek name. Both of the words mean "gazelle" which is kind of like a deer. The Bible was originally written in these two languages, the Old Testament in Hebrew, and the New Testament in Greek! I am thankful for the people who translated the Bible into English from these two languages so that I can read it and understand it!!

What I **LOVE** about this story is the fact that for all the other things that Tabitha could have been known for, she was known as the woman who cared for other people. People loved her because she truly helped other people. She wasn't always thinking about herself and how she could get attention for herself. **NO**! She thought of others first and how she could help them. That is the kind of attention I want!

We all love to get attention. But God wants us to be confident in Him, and not need to get so much attention from other people. When we know that God loves us, and that He thinks we are the most amazing girl in the world, we don't need to grab all the attention we can get from other people. We can feel strong and beautiful because we **KNOW** on the inside that we are important and matter to God.

Closing Prayer: *Dear God. I pray that you help me to care for other people and not try and get attention in ways that aren't pleasing to you. Help me to be known for good things. I thank you that you love me and think I'm amazing! Amen.*

Kindergarten and 1st Grade
Group Discussion Questions

1. Tell us about your *Favorite* birthday ever!

2. Why is it so much fun to have birthdays?

   a. We get to spend time with our family and friends

   b. We get presents

   c. People are really nice to us

   d. We get lots of attention on our birthdays!

   e. People tell us how much they love us

3. God doesn't want us to steal all the attention. What are some ways in which we can try and get all the attention focused on us?

   a. Always talking about what we want to talk about

   b. Always making our friends play the things we want to play

   c. Only thinking about what we want to do

   d. Being selfish

   e. Not considering other people's feelings before we do something

   f. Being too loud or talking too much

4. One of these verses we read today said that "*women should dress modestly…*" What does the word modest mean? (*Ok small group leader… you're gonna need to just be really honest here. These girls need a Godly leader to talk to them about this stuff. Don't be legalistic – but gently and age appropriately address this topic. Good luck!*)

   a. It means to wear clothes that aren't too sassy

   b. We shouldn't wear clothes that look too grown up and make people look at us in a negative way.

   c. We want to make sure our shorts and skirts aren't too short and that our shirts cover up our chest.

169

5. Tabitha was known for the good things she did and how she took care of other people. What are some good things *YOU* are known for?

  a. Being a good friend

  b. Helping my mom and dad

  c. Being kind to others

  d. Sharing my toys

Polka Dot Talk

2nd and 3rd Grade Group Discussion Questions

1. Tell us about your *Favorite* birthday ever!

2. Why is it so much fun to have birthdays?

   a. We get to spend time with our family and friends

   b. We get presents

   c. People are really nice to us

   d. We get lots of attention on our birthdays!

   e. People tell us how much they love us

3. God doesn't want us to steal all the attention. What are some ways in which we can try and get all the attention focused on us?

   a. Always talking about what we want to talk about

   b. Always making our friends play the things we want to play

   c. Only thinking about what we want to do

   d. Being selfish

   e. Not considering other people's feelings before we do something

   f. Being too loud or talking too much

4. One of the verses we read today said that "*women should dress modestly…*" What does the word modest mean? (*Ok small group leader… you're gonna need to just be really honest here. These girls need a Godly leader to talk to them about this stuff. Don't be legalistic – but gently and age appropriately address this topic. Good luck!*)

   a. It means to wear clothes that aren't too sassy

   b. We shouldn't wear clothes that look too grown up and make people look at us in a negative way.

   c. We want to make sure our shorts and skirts aren't too short and that our shirts cover up our chest.

5. Tabitha was known for the good things she did and how she took care of other people. What are some good things *YOU* are known for?

a. Being a good friend

b. Helping my mom and dad

c. Being kind to others

d. Sharing my toys

4th and 5th Grade
Group Discussion Questions

1. Why is it so much fun to have birthdays?

   a. We get to spend time with our family and friends

   b. We get presents

   c. People are really nice to us

   d. We get lots of attention on our birthdays!

   e. People tell us how much they love us

2. God doesn't want us to steal all the attention. What are some ways in which we can try and get all the attention focused on us?

   a. Always talking about what we want to talk about

   b. Always making our friends do the things we want to do

   c. Only thinking about what we want to do

   d. Being selfish

   e. Not considering other people's feelings before we do something

   f. Being too loud or talking too much

   g. Getting in fights to get attention

3. One of the verses we read today said that "*women should dress modestly...*" What does the word modest mean? (*Ok small group leader... you're gonna need to just be really honest here. These girls need a Godly leader to talk to them about this stuff. Don't be legalistic – but gently and age appropriately address this topic. Good luck!*)

   a. It means to wear clothes that aren't too sassy

   b. We shouldn't wear clothes that look too grown up and make people look at us in a negative way.

   c. Share with the girls the following Fashion Tests:

1. Do my shirts show too much belly? Stand up straight, raise your hands like you're worshipping God. If your belly shows, your shirt is too short.
2. We want to make sure our shorts and skirts aren't too short. Look in a mirror and do the following with shorts, skirts and pants:
   a. Sit criss cross
   b. Cross your legs
   c. Bend over and touch your knees
   d. If you can see your undies in the mirror, then your shorts or skirt are too short.
   e. If you can see the top of your undies in the mirror, then your pants are too low.
3. Bend over and ask a parent or friend if they can see your chest? If so, your shirt is too low.

4. Sometimes, when you are in 4th and 5th grade, some girls start to really want to get attention from boys. Have you experienced this? (*Leaders: feel free to open up the discussion here with open ended questions. This age is already venturing down this path (gulp!) and we want to help them from focusing too much on this area*)

   a. God wants you to have lots of good friends who are girls *and* boys! But sometimes trying to get attention from boys can cause us to do crazy things. God doesn't want you to spend *so* much time trying to get attention from boys – he wants you to focus on being a good friend and being known for your kindness!

5. Tabitha was known for the good things she did and how she took care of other people. What are some good things *YOU* are known for?
   a. Being a good friend
   b. Helping my mom and dad
   c. Being kind to others

Tabitha's Necklace

(RECOMMENDED FOR K-2ND GRADE)

Supplies Needed:

- 18" piece of purple yarn or string
- Macaroni Noodles

What Should We Do Next?

- Thread macaroni on the yarn to make a necklace.

Tabitha wasn't always thinking about herself and how she could get attention for herself. She thought of others first and how she could help them. The purple yarn/string is a reminder of the purple cloth Tabitha used to sew clothing for the poor. Wear this necklace as a reminder to think of others before yourself.

Polka Dot PROJECT

Tabitha's Treat Purse
(RECOMMENDED FOR 3RD-5TH GRADE)

Supplies Needed:

- Fun Foam Hearts (6 ½ x 6") – two per girl or Purple Cardstock
- Heart Template (if using cardstock)
- Hole-Punch
- Large Paper Clips
- Ribbon or String
- Scissors
- Gel Pen, Marker or Glitter Glue
- Pretty Embellishments or beads (optional)
- Small Candy Treats

Prep:

- If using cardstock, copy heart template onto cardstock and cut out the hearts.
- Use a paper clip to hold the two hearts together firmly.
- Use a hole-punch to punch holes around the shapes (through both layers), but do **NOT** punch all the way around the top of the heart.

What Should We Do Next?

- "Sew" the heart shapes together with the ribbon or string.
- Leaving enough ribbon or string at the top of the heart to tie together as a handle.
- With a marker, gel pen or glitter glue; decorate the front of the heart.
- Optional: Glue pretty embellishments for extra decoration
- Optional: Thread beads onto the handle.
- Fill the heart with candy.
- Show kindness to someone, like Tabitha, and give the heart filled with candy to a friend or family member.

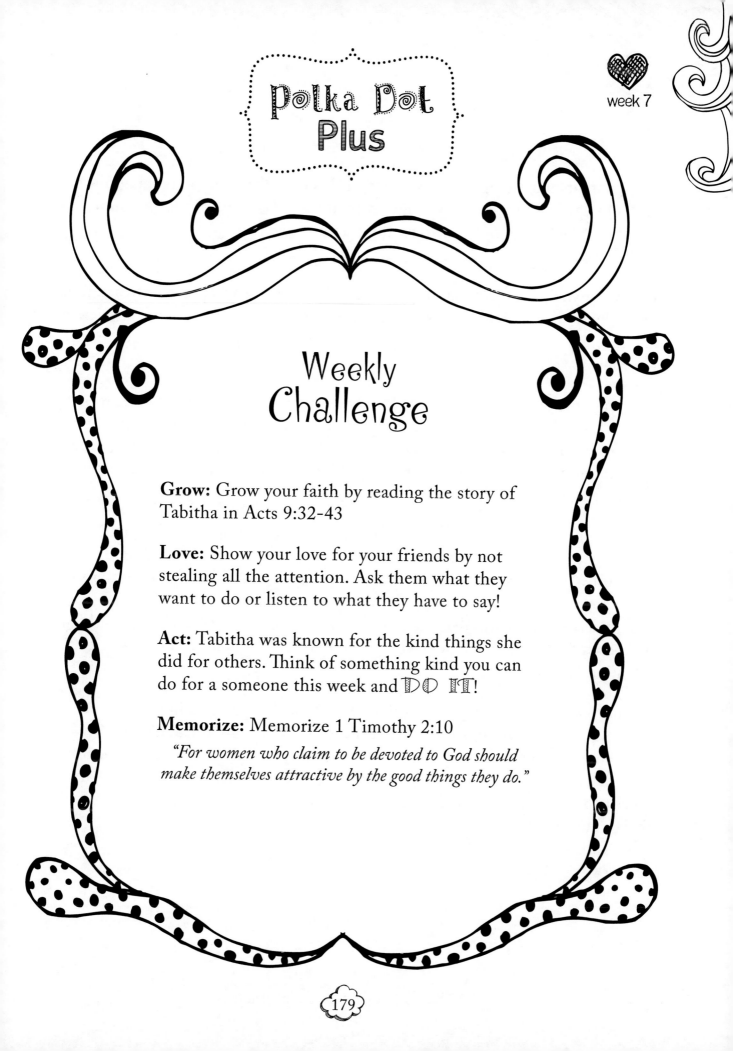

Weekly Challenge

Grow: Grow your faith by reading the story of Tabitha in Acts 9:32-43

Love: Show your love for your friends by not stealing all the attention. Ask them what they want to do or listen to what they have to say!

Act: Tabitha was known for the kind things she did for others. Think of something kind you can do for a someone this week and DO IT!

Memorize: Memorize 1 Timothy 2:10

"For women who claim to be devoted to God should make themselves attractive by the good things they do."

Parent Partner

Well, parents, I'm being a little sneaky on this one. You see, I am seeing more and more girls, younger and younger who are REALLY into boys. I have had countless discussions with my daughters about how boy crazy many of their friends are.

But when you're writing a study that spans kindergarten to pre-teen years, it can be tricky to discuss such topics because there is such a wide span of experience and interest. And so, I prayed and prayed and prayed and I felt like God gave me the topic of "attention."

You see most of the time, when girls are prematurely interested in boys, it isn't really about the boys – it's about the way they feel when they get special attention from someone. In this lesson we discussed that it indeed does feel good to get attention from other people, but that God wants us to focus on Him and not to worry so much about getting attention from other people.

We specifically addressed the attention topic in three ways. First, be a good friend by not stealing all the attention. Secondly, don't try to get attention by doing negative things. We used this point to address modesty, not saying or doing things we know are wrong just to get attention, and in the discussion time for the 4th and 5th graders, we actually talked about… gulp… boys. Lastly, we encouraged them to be known for the kind and good things they do for others instead of trying to get attention for themselves.

My prayer is that you would continue to have really open and honest discussions with your daughters about what it means to be a good friend and how to be friends with boys without diving into romantic relationships too soon. And my prayer is that they would be SO grounded in confidence of who they are in Christ that they would not fall into the trap of looking to relationships to find their value and worth.

Polka Dot Plus

Kindergarten and 1st Grade
Take Home Activity Sheet

Tabitha was known as the woman who cared for other people. People loved her because she truly helped other people. She wasn't always thinking about herself and how she could get attention for herself.

Draw a picture of yourself helping someone!

Like Tabitha, God wants us to think of others above ourselves.

Fill in the missing letters in the verse below by substituting each number with the letter in the key to discover God's message.

For w_____men who claim to be _____evoted to _____ _____ _____
　　　2　　　　　　　　　　3　　　　　　1　　2　　3

should make themselves attractive by the _____ _____ _____ _____ things
　　　　　　　　　　　　　　　　　　　1　　2　　2　　3

they _____ _____. – 1 Timothy 2:10 NLT
　　　3　　2

KEY

G O D
1 2 3

2nd and 3rd Grade
Take Home Activity Sheet

1. Read the amazing story of Tabitha in Acts 9:36-43 in your NIV Bible.
2. Fill in the missing words.
3. Find the missing words in the Word Search puzzle.

'In Joppa there was a disciple named _____ (which,

when translated, is _____), who was always doing

_____ and _____ the poor. About

that time she became sick and died, and her body was washed and placed in an

_____ room.

_____ was near Joppa; so when the disciples heard that

_____ was in Lydda, they sent two men to him and urged him,

'Please come at once!'

Peter went with them, and when he arrived he was taken upstairs to the room.

All the _____ stood around him, crying and showing

him the _____ and other clothing that Dorcas had

_____ while she was still with them.

Peter sent them all out of the room; then he got down on his knees and

_____. Turning toward the dead woman, he said, 'Tabitha,

get up.' She _____ her eyes, and seeing Peter she sat up. He

took her by the _____ and helped her to her feet. Then he

called the _____ and the widows and presented her to them

_____. This became known all over Joppa, and many people

believed in the _____. Peter stayed in Joppa for some time with a

tanner named Simon."

Word Search Puzzle

```
Z V R S R D R O B E S L A F O P
O F K O P E Y O R W Y A N S D E
X T L D E N E P O D T F F Z E C
T C D M M E Z D D G N N L T E E
E G O Q S R I A T S P U T A M R
C O R D R W H H R G N I B F E O
D E C J L T P E T E R C Z E Z E
R H U T I E V L A S F K V O S W
C L S B R E F P D H D I S K M I
D N A H I L S I R O L Y B X X T
S T K L R K O N O A E D A M G O
O T E V O S F G L J Y Z T R G Z
I B S P M K E N X D J E L O D L
H O M E T H E Z R F O I D R S E
K Y E N N I C E G I E Z S T O G
U A J P X H O S E R S C Z C A E
```

Word List

Tabitha	good	helping	upstairs	alive
widows	believers	robes	made	opened
hand	prayed	Lydda	Lord	Dorcus
Peter				

Polka Dot Girls ❧ Relationships

4th and 5th Grade
Take Home Activity Sheet

Step 1: Read the amazing story of Tabitha in Acts 9:36-43 in your NIV Bible and fill in the missing words.

"In Joppa there was a disciple named _____ *(which,*

when translated, is _____*), who was always doing*

_____ *and* _____ *the poor. About*

that time she became sick and died, and her body was washed and placed in an

_____ *room.*

_____ *was near Joppa; so when the disciples heard that*

_____ *was in Lydda, they sent two men to him and urged him,*

'Please come at once!'

Peter went with them, and when he arrived he was taken upstairs to the room.

All the _____ *stood around him, crying and showing*

him the _____ *and other clothing that Dorcas had*

_____ *while she was still with them.*

Peter sent them all out of the room; then he got down on his knees and

_____. *Turning toward the dead woman, he said, 'Tabitha,*

get up.' She _____ her eyes, and seeing Peter she sat up. He

took her by the _____ and helped her to her feet. Then he

called the _____ and the widows and presented her to them

_____. This became known all over Joppa, and many people

believed in the _____. Peter stayed in Joppa for some time with a

tanner named Simon."

Step 2: Find the missing words in the Word Search Puzzle.

```
D  W  S  E  D  S  H  U  O  U  L  D  P  B  E
K  E  N  U  O  N  P  W  S  N  E  R  F  O  R
T  H  N  E  C  S  A  R  G  O  A  D  D  Y  L
O  D  T  E  T  R  E  H  H  Y  R  I  A  N  G
S  W  E  A  P  V  O  D  E  O  O  A  N  M  D
N  O  I  T  E  O  T  D  B  R  Y  T  O  G  E
T  R  A  I  T  T  E  E  N  T  P  I  O  N  F
S  R  L  O  M  T  S  H  E  T  H  E  I  N  G
S  E  V  I  L  A  W  E  W  E  A  R  T  T  R
B  H  E  L  P  I  N  G  Y  I  N  A  S  E  G
D  O  O  G  T  O  B  E  T  H  B  E  W  C  R
L  E  N  T  E  R  O  F  A  I  T  T  O  E  N
T  O  I  O  N  O  R  D  T  O  I  N  D  G  N
E  G  R  A  T  I  V  H  E  T  H  I  I  N  G
S  V  B  D  Z  G  A  J  U  Y  E  Q  W  E  J
```

WORD LIST

alive	*believers*	*Dorcus*	*good*	*hand*
helping	*Lord*	*Lydda*	*made*	*opened*
Peter	*prayed*	*robes*	*Tabitha*	*upstairs*
widows				

Mean Girls

WHAT'S THE POINT?

DON'T BE A MEAN GIRL. AND LOVE THE MEAN GIRLS IN YOUR LIFE.

theme verse

"Love your enemies! Do good to those who hate you.
Bless those who curse you. Pray for those who hurt you."
Luke 6:27-28

related bible story

King David
Psalm 55

 ❀ Large Group Lesson ❀

Sometimes girls are mean.

And it really stinks.

Remember we talked earlier about God's super secret weapon in how to deal with relationships? What was the verse? *"Treat people in the same way that you want them to treat you."* – Luke 6:31 CEB

So – wouldn't it just be the most amazing thing in the world if everyone else treated YOU the way that they wanted to be treated?! If they only spoke kind words to you and never picked on you and never got mad at you? I think that would be ah-mazing.

But unfortunately, that's not the way things are. Even if you are kind and loving, there will be moments when other people say mean things, treat you poorly, and generally make life stink.

Alannah had so much fun playing with the girls on her street… most of the time. Some days they could have the best time 𝔼𝕍𝔼ℝ, and then the next day the girls would get mad at her and leave her house angry and say all kinds of mean things to her. She never really knew what to expect when she was going out to spend time with those girls.

And the 𝕎𝕆ℝ𝕊𝕋 part was that she was starting to see herself behaving in the same way. She got tired of always being the one yelled at, so she started yelling back. It seemed like the only way to get them to listen to her was if she did the same things to them that they were doing to her. But in her heart she knew that this wasn't the way that good friends treated one another.

So – what should Alannah do? And what should you and I do when we're in a situation where it seems like there is 𝕃𝕆𝕋𝕊 of drama and fighting and maybe even someone picking on us for no reason? What does God want us to do?

Well, thankfully, God gives us some answers in the Bible to help us deal with all of these situations. I'm not saying that it will be easy… but doing the right thing is very rarely easy.

First of all,

➡ **1. Don't Do Drama!**

We have a saying at our house whenever anyone is going to play with friends. We say, "Don't Do Drama!" Now what in the world does that mean? Well, when you're with your friends, sometimes things can get tense pretty quick. Just like what Alannah was having with her friends! One friend gets mad at the other friend because the other friend didn't do what the one friend wanted to do and so the first friend storms out of the house saying, "I'm not going to be your friend anymore" and the other friend yells back, "Well, you're not coming to my birthday party then" and then the other friend starts crying and runs to tell her

Mom that her friend is being mean and then the other friend starts crying because she's afraid she's going to get in trouble when it was really the other friend who started it all.........and it goes on and on and on. You know what all THAT is called? Drama! When you get upset easily... it's drama. When you make a huge scene over a little thing... it's drama. When you say mean things to your friend... it's drama.

So, instead of having these crazy fights with your friends all the time, what if you decided to just "Don't Do Drama?!" What that means is that instead of getting emotional and reacting in such a BIG way when your friend does something you don't like, you just calmly talk it out. When your friend says something that upsets you, instead of coming back at her with something just as sassy, what if you just said, "I'm sorry you feel that way, how can we work this out?"

Proverbs 29:11 says, "*A foolish person lets his anger run wild. But a wise person keeps himself under control.*" (NIRV) You can get angry and frustrated, but learn to talk about things with your friends and work them out calmly without all the drama. Cause you know what, the drama just makes everything worse.

SO – next time you are having a disagreement with your friend, and you are tempted to start getting emotional and angry, say to yourself "Don't Do Drama" and find a calm way to talk through your issues.

(Oh yeah... and if your friend continues to "DO DRAMA" even when you're trying not to, don't give up. Just ignore it and move onto something else. It's takes two people to have a fight and if you simply don't dive into the mess, she will eventually calm down too!!)

The second thing we need to remember when dealing with mean people is,

➡ 2. Love your enemies.

Casey was picked on by a girl at school *all the time*. She made fun of her clothes. She made fun of her school work. She made fun of her family. She talked about her to other people. She made Casey's life *miserable*.

She didn't know what to do. She talked to her Mom about it, and they met with her teacher and the other girl and her parents. She was really embarrassed, but she knew that it was important to tell a grown up what was going on.

After the meeting, things got better, but something in Casey's heart got worse. She was SO angry at this girl. How could someone treat another person that way? Why did she do those things? Inside, she just wanted to get back at her. But she knew that God wanted her to forgive the person who had hurt her. She knew that the Bible said, "*Love your enemies! Do good to those who hate you. Bless those who curse you. Pray for those who hurt you.*" (Luke 6:27-28)

So, she asked God to help her love her enemy. She began to pray for the person who had hurt her so badly. She showed kindness to her, even though she really wanted to punch her in the face! And she didn't say bad things about her to other people.

Something amazing happened when Casey decided to do what the Bible said. Her heart began to feel better. She didn't feel as angry any more. Actually, God softened her heart so that she could see that this girl was really just scared and insecure.

Now, it's not like she suddenly wanted to be her best friend! And she didn't start hanging out with her or anything like that. She didn't even really LIKE her. But God helped her love her by seeing her as one of God's daughters… just like she was. She knew that God loved this girl – and so she could love her and pray that she would get to know Jesus and that He would change her heart.

God will help you love your enemies.

But, what about another groups of people? What about people who USED to be your friends and now they won't be your friend anymore?

⟹ 3. Ask God to help you with broken relationships.

It's one thing to have a stranger pick on you and be mean to you… but it's a whole other thing when someone who USED to be a close friend suddenly won't be your friend anymore and is mean to you. I think this is one of the most painful things we can experience in our relationships. It is REALLY hard when our relationships are broken and someone who used to be our friend is now the person who is hurting us.

I think it hurts so much because they know so much about you! They were close to you and know what you're really like. It can be really hard because you can feel like you're not good enough. Like someone got to know the real you, and once they got to know you, they just didn't want to be your friend anymore. That is **REALLY, REALLY** painful.

This EXACT thing happened to someone in the Bible. King David writes about it in Psalm 55. He starts out by telling us that someone is **NOT** being very kind to him. He says, "*Listen to my prayer, O God. Do not ignore my cry for help! Please listen and answer me, for I am overwhelmed by my troubles. My enemies shout at me, making loud and wicked threats. They bring trouble on me and angrily hunt me down.*" (Psalm 55:1-3) King David is **NOT** having a good day.

But as we look further on in the chapter, we see **WHO** the person is who is giving him such a hard time! "*This isn't the neighborhood bully mocking me—I could take that. This isn't a foreign devil spitting invective—I could tune that out. It's you! We grew up together! You! My best friend! Those long hours of leisure as we walked arm in arm, God a third party to our conversation.*" (Psalm 55:12-14 MSG)

It's someone who used to be his friend! His best friend!! Can you imagine how sad King David must have felt! The person causing him so much trouble was actually someone who was supposed to be a friend?!

If you have a person who used to be your friend who is now being mean to you, I am really, really sorry, I know that is very hard and I am sorry that this has happened to you. But, you can do exactly what King David did! He asked God to help him. Psalm 55: 16 says, "*But I will call on God, and the Lord will rescue me.*" Ask God to help you know what to do in the situation. Maybe you need to apologize for something. Maybe you need to reach out to them in kindness. Or maybe you just need to let it go and ask God to help you forgive the person who has hurt you.

Man, it's **SO** hard to forgive the people that hurt us. It's hard to let go when everything in us wants to fight back and make them hurt the way we are hurting. But God wants you to forgive others. Colossians 3:13 says, "*Make allowance for each other's faults, and forgive anyone who offends you. Remember, the Lord forgave you, so you must forgive others.*"

Ask God to help you let go of your hurt and anger. Ask Him to help you forgive.

What if you and I decided that we were going to just STOP all the mean girl stuff. What if we just said, "You know what, I will just choose to be a kind girl." If we chose to forgive and love those who hurt us, and always show love and stick up for the girls who are being hurt by other people, we could really change a lot of things.

SO – let's do it! No more mean.

During your craft time tonight, you are going to sign the Polka Dot Girls NO MORE MEAN Treaty. It simply says this:

"I promise, as Polka Dot Girl and as a daughter of God, to treat other girls with kindness and respect. I will not be mean. I will not Do Drama. And I will forgive and love those who are mean to me, instead of being mean back. I will show the love of Jesus in the way I talk, act, and treat my friends."

Closing Prayer: *Dear God, I thank you that you have promised to always be with me no matter what I am going through. I pray you help me know what to do when other girls are being mean to me. I pray you help me to "Don't Do Drama" and to forgive and love those who are mean to me. And I promise that I will be kind and loving to the girls around me, because it will make You happy. I love you, Amen.*

Kindergarten and 1st Grade Group Discussion Questions

1. Have you ever had someone be mean to you? How did that make you feel?

2. Have you ever wanted to be mean back to someone who was mean to you? What does God say we should do?

    a. We shouldn't be mean back.

3. In this lesson we learned to "Don't Do Drama!" What does that mean?

    a. Instead of getting emotional and reacting in such a BIG way when your friend does something you don't like, instead try to calmly talk it out.

    b. When your friend says something that upsets you, instead of coming back at her with something just as sassy, what if you just said, "I'm sorry you feel that way. How can we work this out?"

    c. You can get angry and frustrated, but learn to talk about things with your friends and work them out calmly without all the drama.

    d. Next time you are having a disagreement with your friend, and you are tempted to start getting emotional and angry, say to yourself "Don't Do Drama" and find a calm way to talk through your issues.

    e. And if your friend continues to "DO DRAMA" even when you're trying not to, don't give up. Just ignore it and move onto something else. It's takes two people to have a fight and if you simply don't dive into the mess, she will eventually calm down too!!

4. What should we do if we are being bullied by someone?

    a. Talk to your mom or dad or teacher.

    b. Be kind, but stand up for yourself

5. What does it mean to love your enemies?

   a. We love them because God loves them.

   b. We pray for them

   c. We don't have to be friends with them, but we should be kind.

   d. We have to forgive them for hurting us.

   e. We choose to not talk bad about them to other people.

6. Have you ever had someone who used to be your friend, suddenly become mean and not want to be your friend anymore? How did that make you feel?

7. God says that we need to forgive the friends who hurt us. Practice saying this week's theme verse together. *"Love your enemies! Do good to those who hate you. Bless those who curse you. Pray for those who hurt you."* (Luke 6:27-28)

Polka Dot Talk

2nd and 3rd Grade
Group Discussion Questions

1. Have you ever had someone be mean to you? How did that make you feel?

2. Have you ever wanted to be mean back to someone who was mean to you? What does God say we should do?

   a. We shouldn't be mean back.

3. In this lesson we learned to "Don't Do Drama!" What does that mean?

   a. Instead of getting emotional and reacting in such a BIG way when your friend does something you don't like, instead try to calmly talk it out.

   b. When your friend says something that upsets you, instead of coming back at her with something just as sassy, what if you just said, "I'm sorry you feel that way. How can we work this out?"

   c. You can get angry and frustrated, but learn to talk about things with your friends and work them out calmly without all the drama.

   d. Next time you are having a disagreement with your friend, and you are tempted to start getting emotional and angry, say to yourself "Don't Do Drama" and find a calm way to talk through your issues.

   e. And if your friend continues to "DO DRAMA" even when you're trying not to, don't give up. Just ignore it and move onto something else. It's takes two people to have a fight and if you simply don't dive into the mess, she will eventually calm down too!!

4. What should we do if we are being bullied by someone?

   a. Talk to your mom or dad or teacher.

   b. Be kind, but stand up for yourself

5. What does it mean to love your enemies?

    a. We love them because God loves them.

    b. We pray for them

    c. We don't have to be friends with them, but we should be kind.

    d. We have to forgive them for hurting us.

    e. We choose to not talk bad about them to other people.

6. Have you ever had someone who used to be your friend, suddenly become mean and not want to be your friend anymore? How did that make you feel?

7. God says that we need to forgive the friends who hurt us. Practice saying this week's theme verse together. *"Love your enemies! Do good to those who hate you. Bless those who curse you. Pray for those who hurt you."* (Luke 6:27-28)

Polka Dot Talk

4th and 5th Grade
Group Discussion Questions

1. Have you ever had someone be mean to you? How did that make you feel?

2. Have you ever wanted to be mean back to someone who was mean to you? What does God say we should do?

   a. We shouldn't be mean back.

3. In this lesson we learned to "Don't Do Drama!" What does that mean?

   a. Instead of getting emotional and reacting in such a BIG way when your friend does something you don't like, instead try to talk it out.

   b. When your friend says something that upsets you, instead of coming back at her with something just as sassy, what if you just said, "I'm sorry you feel that way. How can we work this out?"

   c. You can get angry and frustrated, but learn to talk about things with your friends and work them out calmly without all the drama.

   d. Next time you are having a disagreement with your friend, and you are tempted to start getting emotional and angry, say to yourself "Don't Do Drama" and find a calm way to talk through your issues.

   e. And if your friend continues to "DO DRAMA" even when you're trying not to, don't give up. Just ignore it and move onto something else. It's takes two people to have a fight and if you simply don't dive into the mess, she will eventually calm down too!!

4. What should we do if we are being bullied by someone?

   a. Talk to your mom or dad or teacher.

   b. Be kind, but stand up for yourself

5. What does it mean to love your enemies?

   a. We love them because God loves them.

   b. We pray for them

   c. We don't have to be friends with them, but we should be kind.

   d. We have to forgive them for hurting us.

   e. We choose to not talk bad about them to other people.

6. Have you ever had someone who used to be your friend, suddenly become mean and not want to be your friend anymore? How did that make you feel?

7. God says that we need to forgive the friends who hurt us. Practice saying this week's theme verse together. *"Love your enemies! Do good to those who hate you. Bless those who curse you. Pray for those who hurt you."* (Luke 6:27-28)

Polka Dot Talk

4th and 5th Grade
Group Discussion Questions

1. Have you ever had someone be mean to you? How did that make you feel?

2. Have you ever wanted to be mean back to someone who was mean to you? What does God say we should do?

   a. We shouldn't be mean back.

3. In this lesson we learned to "Don't Do Drama!" What does that mean?

   a. Instead of getting emotional and reacting in such a BIG way when your friend does something you don't like, instead try to talk it out.

   b. When your friend says something that upsets you, instead of coming back at her with something just as sassy, what if you just said, "I'm sorry you feel that way. How can we work this out?"

   c. You can get angry and frustrated, but learn to talk about things with your friends and work them out calmly without all the drama.

   d. Next time you are having a disagreement with your friend, and you are tempted to start getting emotional and angry, say to yourself "Don't Do Drama" and find a calm way to talk through your issues.

   e. And if your friend continues to "DO DRAMA" even when you're trying not to, don't give up. Just ignore it and move onto something else. It's takes two people to have a fight and if you simply don't dive into the mess, she will eventually calm down too!!

4. What should we do if we are being bullied by someone?

   a. Talk to your mom or dad or teacher.

   b. Be kind, but stand up for yourself

5. What does it mean to love your enemies?

   a. We love them because God loves them.

   b. We pray for them

   c. We don't have to be friends with them, but we should be kind.

   d. We have to forgive them for hurting us.

   e. We choose to not talk bad about them to other people.

6. Have you ever had someone who used to be your friend, suddenly become mean and not want to be your friend anymore? How did that make you feel?

7. God says that we need to forgive the friends who hurt us. Practice saying this week's theme verse together. *"Love your enemies! Do good to those who hate you. Bless those who curse you. Pray for those who hurt you."* (Luke 6:27-28)

Polka Dot Girls NO MORE MEAN Treaty

Supplies Needed:

- *No More Mean Treaty* Template
- White Cardstock
- Color Crayons/Markers
- Black Poster Board or 12 x 12 Black Cardstock
- 8 ½ x 11" Sheets of Scrapbook Paper
- Scissors or Paper Cutter
- Glue Stick or Elmer's Glue
- Pretty Embellishments
- Ribbon – 12 inches/girl
- Masking Tape

Prep:

- Copy No More Mean Treaty Template onto white cardstock.
- Trim the cardstock along the cut line.
- Cut Poster Board or Black Cardstock into 9 ½ x 12" sections.
- Cut Ribbon.

What Should We Do Next?

- Mount scrapbook paper onto black poster board with Elmer's glue.
- Color the *No More Mean Treaty*.
- Sign the *No More Mean Treaty*.
- Mount the *No More Mean Treaty* onto the scrapbook paper.
- Decorate your frame with pretty embellishments (buttons, flowers, stickers, glitter.)
- Attach the ribbon onto the back of the poster board with masking tape.
- Hang the signed treaty in your room to remind yourself to follow the Polka Dot Girl *No More Mean Treaty*!

I promise, as a Polka Dot Girl

and as a daughter of God,

to treat other girls with kindness and respect.

I will not be mean!

I will not Do Drama!

And I will forgive and love those who are mean to me,
instead of being mean back.

I will show the love of Jesus in the way
I talk, act, and treat my friends.

Signed by: _____

Date: _____

Polka Dot Plus

Weekly Challenge

Grow: Grow by reading the story of King David in Psalm 55.

Love: Practice loving your enemies this week. Each night, say a prayer for someone who has been mean to you. Pray for God to bless them.

Act: Practice "Don't Do Drama!" When you are with your friends, refuse to get let things get ugly. Practice talking through your problems without getting too upset.

Memorize: Memorize this week's theme verse:

"Love your enemies! Do good to those who hate you. Bless those who curse you. Pray for those who hurt you."
Luke 6:27-28

Parent Partner

Oh how I wish it wasn't true. I wish that our girls wouldn't ever have to deal with "mean girls." But the reality of life is that at one point or another, your daughter will have to deal with some female drama.

We taught your girls a saying that we often say at our house: "Don't Do Drama!" I say this to our girls whenever they are leaving the house and about to spend time with their friends. This means, don't get too worked up about stuff and get angry and then say you're not going to be someone's friend anymore… you know the drill. Instead, we want them to simply work through their disagreements and differences calmly without it escalating into a "drama fest!"

Secondly, we talked to them about loving their enemies. God wants us to love and pray for the people who hurt us. Now, this doesn't mean you have to be friends with these people, but God wants us to love them in our hearts. We talked about bullying, and that they should tell their parents if something is going on at school or in your neighborhood. But to keep their hearts from getting hardened, they have to forgive those who have hurt them.

And lastly, we discussed friendships that have been broken. Many times girls who used to be the closest of friends can suddenly find themselves in a relationship totally broken. Many times, our daughters may not even know what happened – they just know that someone who used to be their friend doesn't want to be their friend anymore.

Again, we encouraged them to come to Jesus with their hurt and pray that God will give them wisdom as to how to deal with the situation. (You may need to pray for wisdom for this too!!) We taught them to forgive their friend and refuse to be mean back.

Kindergarten and 1st Grade
Take Home Activity Sheet

What should you do when we're in a situation where it seems like there is **LOTS** of drama and fighting and maybe even someone picking on us for no reason? The following scripture instructs us how to treat people who hurt us.

Step 1: Find the hidden words from the list in the Word Search Puzzle.

Step 2: Place the hidden words in the correct blank in the scripture verse.

Step 3: Go to your Bible and find Luke 6:27-28 NLT to check your answer.

"_____ *your enemies! Do* _____

to those who hate you. _____ *those who curse you.*

_____ *for those who hurt you.*" – Luke 6:27-28 NLT

WORD SEARCH PUZZLE

N	O	O	T	B	B
V	T	A	F	M	L
P	E	E	G	U	E
R	S	F	O	V	S
A	F	S	O	X	S
Y	D	L	D	M	T

WORD LIST

bless   *love*   *good*   *pray*

2nd and 3rd Grade
Take Home Activity Sheets

Jesus died on the cross so that the sins of all people could be forgiven. He did this out of love.

Solve the puzzle to find out what God wants us to do for the people who have hurt us.

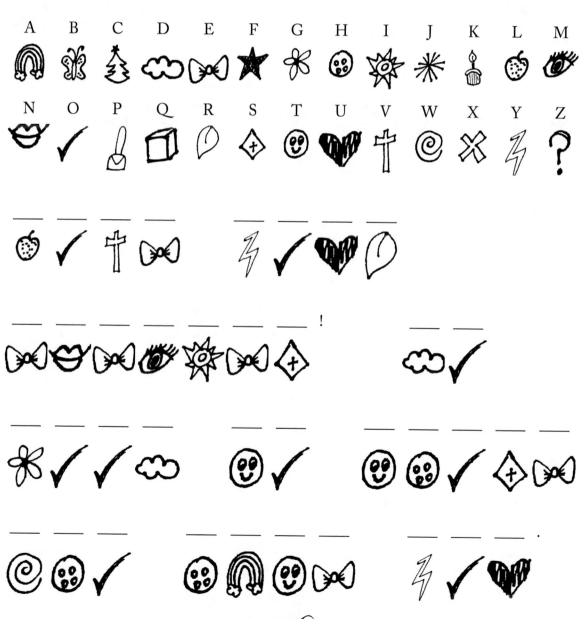

_____ _____ _____ _____ 6:26-27 NLT

Answer: _Love your enemies! Do good to those who hate you. Bless those who curse you. Pray for those who hurt you._ Luke 6:26-27 NLT

4th and 5th Grade
Take Home Activity Sheets

Look up the Bible passages below and fill in the blank lines with the missing letters.

When you have filled in all the blank lines, put the circled letters in the matching numbered lines to find out what God wants us to do for the people who have hurt us. All scripture NIV

A fool gives full ⃝ ___ ___ ⃝ *to his anger, but a wise man keeps himself*
            3   15

under control. – Proverbs 29:11

Do to ⃝ ___ ___ ___ ___ ___ *as you would have them do to you.* – Luke 6:31
   2

But I ___ ___ ⃝ ___ *to God, and the* ___ ___ ___ ⃝ *saves me.*
              1   7

– Psalm 55:16

Bear with each other and ⃝ ⃝ ___ ___ ___ ___ ⃝ *whatever*
                              12 13   4,17

grievances you may have against one another. Forgive as the Lord forgave you.
– Colossians 3:13

And when you stand ⃝ ___ ⃝ ___ ___ ⃝ ___ *, if you hold*
                     8   5,10   6

anything against anyone, forgive him, so that your Father in heaven may forgive you your sins. – Mark 11:25

Lord, how many times shall I forgive ⃝ ___
                                         18

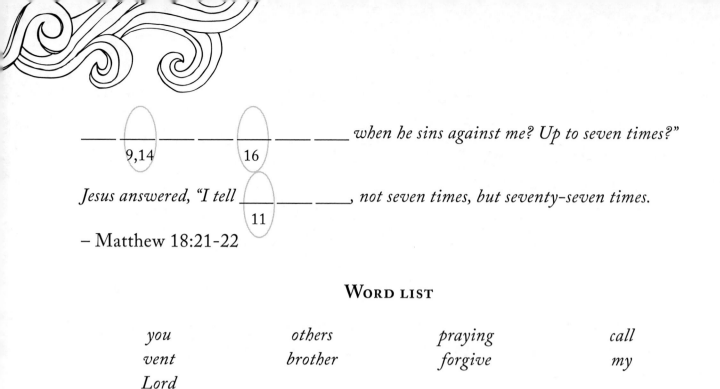

_____ ⟨_____⟩ _____ ⟨_____⟩ _____ _____ *when he sins against me? Up to seven times?"*

9,14   16

Jesus answered, "I tell ⟨_____⟩ _____ _____*, not seven times, but seventy-seven times.*

11

– Matthew 18:21-22

Word list

you	*others*	*praying*	*call*
vent	*brother*	*forgive*	*my*
Lord			

God's instruction is to:

_____ _____ _____ _____   _____ _____ _____   _____ _____ _____ _____
 1   2   3   4   5   6   7   8   9   10   11

_____ _____ _____   _____ _____ _____ _____.
 12   13   14   15   16   17   18

Relationships

Do The Right Thing

WHAT'S THE POINT?
GOD WANTS YOU TO STAND UP FOR WHAT IS RIGHT.

theme verse

"Do what is right. Then you will be accepted. If you don't do what is right, sin is waiting at your door to grab you. It longs to have you. But you must rule over it."

Genesis 4:7 NIRV

related bible story

King Josiah
2 Kings 22

❀ Large Group Lesson ❀

We have talked this entire series about how important our relationships are. God has blessed us with incredible friends and family who walk through our lives with us. They remind us that we are not alone and they can help us become the very best we can be!

But sometimes our relationships can become so important to us that we are willing to do anything to make the people in our lives happy.

Sophia loved spending time with her friends. One day, she was at the store with her friend Carmen. Suddenly, she saw Carmen take a piece of candy from the shelf and put it in her pocket without paying for it. Sophia couldn't believe it!

Then it got worse. Carmen took another piece of candy and put it in Sophia's pocket too. Sophia didn't know what to do. She knew that it was wrong to steal, but she didn't want her friend to get mad at her. She didn't say anything and then spent the rest of the day feeling sick to her stomach.

Sometimes our friends try to get us to do things that we know we shouldn't do. Sometimes our friends say things that we know aren't pleasing to God. And sometimes our friends can behave in a way that we KNOW isn't right.

What should we do in those moments? Does a good friend just overlook those things and not say anything? Or does a good friend stand up for what is right?

The answer is ALWAYS that a good friend stands up for what is right. A good friend wants their friends to make right choices and sometimes that means we have to speak up when your friends are doing something that is wrong. And even if that means your friend gets mad at you or EVEN says that they won't be your friend anymore, it is better for you to do what is right.

POLKA DOT POINTERS

If someone tells you that they aren't going to be your friend anymore if you don't do what they tell you – even if it's something you don't want to you or something you know is wrong – then that person isn't a very good friend. GOOD friends don't make other people do things they know are wrong. And good friends always help you make good choices, not bad ones. Make sure you surround yourself with good friends!

week 9

But this can be REALLY hard! Reeeeeeallllyyy hard. No one likes to have their friends upset with them. It's not easy to speak up when everyone else is just going along with what is going on. And it is very hard to stand up and do what is right when everyone else is doing what is wrong.

But God always wants you to do the right thing. He asks us to stand up and not just go along with the things our friends are doing that we know are wrong. 1 Peter 3:14 says, *"But even if you suffer for doing what is right, God will reward you for it. So don't worry or be afraid of their threats."* Even when we are scared of what our friends might say, we need to honor God by doing what is right.

How do we do this? How can we get the courage to do the right thing even when we feel HUGE pressure to just go along with what everyone else is doing?

First of all, we need to

⇒ 1. Live to please God.

Sophia really liked her friend Carmen. She always sat with her at lunch and walked home from school with her. Sophia hated the idea of Carmen being mad at her and she couldn't imagine what it would be like if Carmen wouldn't be her friend.

But in her heart, she knew that what Carmen was doing was wrong. She knew that she shouldn't take things that she hadn't paid for and that it wouldn't please her parents and especially that it wouldn't please God.

But the problem was that Sophia was more worried about what her FRIEND would think than what GOD would think. She was more worried about making her FRIEND happy than making GOD happy. She didn't want her FRIEND to be upset with her, but she wasn't so worried about making GOD upset that she didn't steal the candy. Proverbs 29:25 says, *"Fearing people is a dangerous trap, but to trust in the Lord means safety."*

What would have given Sophia the courage to do the right thing? She should have been more worried about pleasing GOD than pleasing her friend. Even though she was scared that her friend would be mad at her, she should have been MORE concerned with doing something that God says is wrong.

213

Girls, we HAVE to care more about what God thinks than ANYONE ELSE. We have to do the things that will make HIM happy even if it means our friends might be upset with us. Choosing the right thing always pleases God. And we have to live to please God instead of pleasing other people.

The times when we fail to stand up for what is right, we are usually more concerned with pleasing our friends than we are about pleasing God. John 12:43 talks about some people who were having this EXACT problem. It says, "*For they loved human praise more than the praise of God.*" People were making wrong choices because they wanted to make people happy MORE than they wanted to make God happy.

Make the decision today that you are ALWAYS going to do the thing that will please God. Make HIM first in your life, and in the moments when you are feeling scared to stand up to your friends, you will KNOW in your heart that you HAVE to please God more than other people.

Galatians 1:10 says, "*If I were still trying to please men, I would not be Christ's servant.*" Let's be girls who are servants of Christ and live to please HIM instead of other people!

The second way we can stand up for what is right is to,

⇨ 2. Know what the Bible says, and then DO it!

There's a story in the Bible about a young man named Josiah. Josiah became the King of Judah when he was 8 years old!! Can you imagine?!? The years before Josiah became King, the other leaders of Judah had decided to walk away from God. They didn't do all the things the Bible told them to do anymore. Actually, Josiah didn't even KNOW about the law and the commands of God! His parents hadn't taught Him about the things that God said were right and wrong.

But Josiah had a heart that wanted to please God. One day, Josiah's high priest discovered the scrolls in the Temple that had the laws of God written on them. The high priest told Josiah what the law said and Josiah became very upset because he realized that all the people were not doing the things that God had asked them to do. He said this to the high priest, *"Go to the Temple and speak to the Lord for me and for the people and for all Judah. Inquire about the words written in this scroll that has been found. For the Lord's great anger is burning against us because our ancestors have not obeyed the words in this scroll. We have not been doing everything it says we must do."* (2 Kings 22:13)

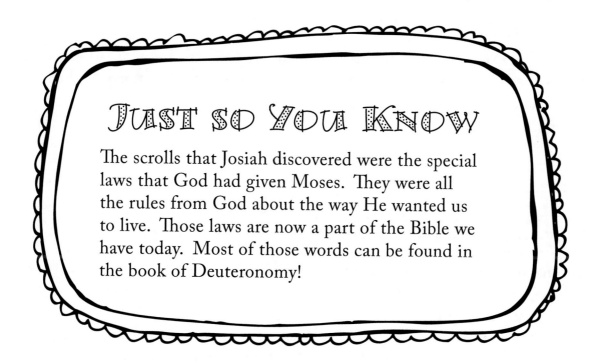

JUST SO YOU KNOW

The scrolls that Josiah discovered were the special laws that God had given Moses. They were all the rules from God about the way He wanted us to live. Those laws are now a part of the Bible we have today. Most of those words can be found in the book of Deuteronomy!

Once Josiah understood the way that God wanted him and all the people of Judah to live, he went to work. He tore down all the idols in the land because the law told him to. He had the people say they were sorry for their behavior, because the scrolls told him to. He made all the changes that the law told him to make because he wanted to honor God. 2 Kings 22:2 says this about Josiah: *"He did what was pleasing in the Lord's sight and followed the example of his ancestor David. He did not turn away from doing what was right."*

If you're going to do the things that God wants you to do, then you need to know the Bible! Josiah wasn't doing the things that God wanted – simply because He didn't know any better! You need to read your Bible and learn the things that God say we should do. And we should also read the Bible to learn the things that God says we shouldn't do!

The Bible is so amazing. It can give us wisdom and insight in so many areas of our lives. It can help us know how to be a kind friend, a good daughter, a hard worker, and many, many other things. 2 Timothy 3:16 says, "*All Scripture is inspired by God and is useful to teach us what is true and to make us realize what is wrong in our lives. It corrects us when we are wrong and teaches us to do what is right.*"

God will show you the right way to live your life through the words He wrote to you in the Bible. BUT- you have to read it and learn what it says!! That's why it's so important to read your Bible every day – so you can know the things God wants you to do!

And the last way you can do the right thing is to

⇒ 3. Be a leader.

When Josiah discovered the law, he quickly changed the things in his own life that weren't pleasing to God. But he did even more than that! He led the other people in his nation back to the ways of God.

God wants you to make the right choices and He wants you to help LEAD other people into the right choices as well. There will come a moment sometime in your life when a group of friends is heading for a wrong choice. Maybe everyone at a slumber party is watching something they shouldn't be watching or a group of friends is being mean to someone. In those moments, you have a choice. You can go along with what everyone else is doing, or you can stand up and be a leader! Instead of following other people down the wrong path, you can stand up and lead your friends down the RIGHT path!

God doesn't want you to follow other people. He wants you to be a leader! He doesn't want you to do whatever other people say, even when you know it's wrong. He wants you to lead your friends into doing the right thing!

There is a verse in Deuteronomy that talks about being a leader. It says, "*If you listen to these commands of the Lord your God that I am giving you today, and if you carefully obey them, the Lord will make you the head and not the tail, and you will always be on top and never at the bottom.*" – Deuteronomy 28:13

It might sound funny, but when my kids are leaving the house to go play with their friends, do you know what I say to them? I tell them, "You are the head and not the tail." What does that mean? Well, think about a puppy. He's running around all cute and cuddly and wagging his tail. What is deciding where that puppy is going to go: his head or his tail? His HEAD! What is deciding what that puppy is going to do: his head or his tail? His HEAD. The head is the leader of the dog. The tail just follows behind.

You and I are the head and not the tail! We should be leading our friends into GOOD things, not following our friends into bad things. We should not follow our friends into doing things we know will not please God. We should lead our friends into things that we know are right! YOU are the head and not the tail. You are a leader, not a follower. You can choose the RIGHT thing instead of following people into the wrong thing!!

God wants you to stand up for what is right. Genesis 4:7 says, "*Do what is right. Then you will be accepted. If you don't do what is right, sin is waiting at your door to grab you. It longs to have you. But you must rule over it.*" (NIRV) You have a choice. You can do the right thing – or you can choose the wrong thing. God is there to help you make the right choices and live a life that honors Him.

Closing Prayer: *Dear God. I want to stand up for the right thing. Help me to want to please You more than I want to please my friends. I will read Your Word and do the things it tells me to do. And I want to be a leader who shows other people how to honor You. Amen.*

Kindergarten and 1st Grade Group Discussion Questions

1. Our friends are really important to us. Have you ever had a friend try to get you to do something you knew was wrong? Share you story with the group.

2. Why is it hard to stand up to our friends when they want us to do something that isn't right?

   a. We don't' want them to get mad at us

   b. We don't want to hurt their feelings

   c. We're scared they won't be our friend anymore if we don't do what they say.

3. Does a good friend just overlook things that are wrong and not say anything? Or does a good friend stand up for what is right?

   a. A good friend ALWAYS stands up for what is right.

4. What does it mean to "live to please God?'

   a. We need to worry more about pleasing God than pleasing our friends.

   b. God should have first place in our lives and we should try to behave in a way that honors Him.

   c. We need to be more concerned with making God happy with us than doing what our friends tell us to do.

5. King Josiah learned what the Bible said and then worked hard to follow the things it told him to do. Is there something you have worked hard to do (or stop doing) because the Bible told you to?

   a. Changed an attitude

   b. Stopped talking bad about a friend

   c. Obeyed their parents

   d. Helped people who didn't have any food or money because the Bible says to do that.

6. The Bible says that "you are the head and not the tail." What does that mean?

    a. You are a leader, not a follower

    b. You shouldn't follow other people by doing things you know are wrong.

    c. You should lead your friends into good things, not follow them in to bad things.

Polka Dot Talk

2nd and 3rd Grade Group Discussion Questions

1. Our friends are really important to us. Have you ever had a friend try to get you to do something you knew was wrong? Share you story with the group.

2. Why is it hard to stand up to our friends when they want us to do something that isn't right?

   a. We don't' want them to get mad at us

   b. We don't want to hurt their feelings

   c. We're scared they won't be our friend anymore if we don't do what they say.

3. Does a good friend just overlook things that are wrong and not say anything? Or does a good friend stand up for what is right?

   a. A good friend ALWAYS stands up for what is right.

4. What does it mean to "live to please God?"

   a. We need to worry more about pleasing God than pleasing our friends.

   b. God should have first place in our lives and we should try to behave in a way that honors Him.

   c. We need to be more concerned with making God happy with us than doing what our friends tell us to do.

5. King Josiah learned what the Bible said and then worked hard to follow the things it told him to do. Is there something you have worked hard to do (or stop doing) because the Bible told you to?

   a. Changed an attitude

   b. Stopped talking bad about a friend

   c. Obeyed their parents

   d. Helped people who didn't have any food or money because the Bible says to do that.

6. The Bible says that "you are the head and not the tail." What does that mean?

   a. You are a leader, not a follower

   b. You shouldn't follow other people by doing things you know are wrong.

   c. You should lead your friends into good things, not follow them in to bad things.

Polka Dot Talk

4th and 5th Grade
Group Discussion Questions

1. Our friends are really important to us. Have you ever had a friend try to get you to do something you knew was wrong? Share you story with the group.

2. Why is it hard to stand up to our friends when they want us to do something that isn't right?

   a. We don't' want them to get mad at us

   b. We don't want to hurt their feelings

   c. We're scared they won't be our friend anymore if we don't do what they say.

3. Does a good friend just overlook things that are wrong and not say anything? Or does a good friend stand up for what is right?

   a. A good friend ALWAYS stands up for what is right.

4. What does it mean to "live to please God?'

   a. We need to worry more about pleasing God than pleasing our friends.

   b. God should have first place in our lives and we should try to behave in a way that honors Him.

   c. We need to be more concerned with making God happy with us than doing what our friends tell us to do.

5. King Josiah learned what the Bible said and then worked hard to follow the things it told him to do. Is there something you have worked hard to do (or stop doing) because the Bible told you to?

   a. Changed an attitude

   b. Stopped talking bad about a friend

   c. Obeyed their parents

   d. Helped people who didn't have any food or money because the Bible says to do that.

6. The Bible says that "you are the head and not the tail." What does that mean?

   a. You are a leader, not a follower

   b. You shouldn't follow other people by doing things you know are wrong.

   c. You should lead your friends into good things, not follow them in to bad things.

"My Scroll"

Supplies Needed:

- Scroll template
- 8 ½ x 11" Paper (recommend light brown or an antique look)
- Crayons and/or Markers
- Pretty Embellishments (stickers, glitter, etc.)
- Pencils
- Ribbon or Raffia

Prep:

- Copy template onto the paper.

What Should We Do Next?

- Color the scroll with crayons and/or makers.
- Gently crinkle up the paper into a ball and then straighten it out several times to make it look old.
- Carefully open up your picture. Run your hand over the picture to straighten out the paper.
- Add pretty embellishments
- Curl the edge of the paper around a pencil and tightly role the entire sheet of paper to create the scroll effect.
- Repeat the step above and curl the other edge of the paper around a pencil and tightly role the entire sheet of paper.
- When complete, roll the curled ends toward the middle and tie with a ribbon or raffia.

"All Scripture is inspired by God and is useful to teach us what is true and to make us realize what is wrong in our lives. It corrects us when we are wrong and teaches us to do what is right." – 2 Timothy 3:16 NLT

1. Live to please God

2. Know what the Bible says and DO it.

3. Be a LEADER!

Polka Dot Plus

Weekly Challenge

Grow – Grow by reading the story of King Josiah in 2 Kings 22.

Love – Be a good friend by helping your friends make the right choices. Speak up even when it's hard and love them even if they get angry with you for doing what is right.

Act – Read your Bible this week and write down some of the things that God says. Start in the book of Proverbs, it is full of wisdom for how to live our lives in a way that pleases God!

Memorize – Memorize this week's theme verse.

"Do what is right. Then you will be accepted. If you don't do what is right, sin is waiting at your door to grab you. It longs to have you. But you must rule over it."

Genesis 4:7 NIRV

Parent Partner

I am constantly praying a very specific prayer over my children. I pray that God will give them the strength and courage to stand up for what is right. I pray that they would have the bravery to go against what everyone else may be doing and choose to make choices that honor God.

This week in Polka Dot Girls, we talked about standing up for what is right. We encouraged the girls to live to please God instead of other people. When they are in a moment of decision, our hope is that they will know in their hearts that they pleasing God is FAR more important than pleasing their friends.

Secondly, we talked about reading the Bible so that we know the way that God wants us to live. It is our instruction manual for life, and God has given us tons of instruction as to how we can live lives that honor God.

And lastly, we encouraged the girls to be leaders, not followers. I always look my kids in the eyes before they leave the house and say, "You are the head and not the tail!" This is based on Deuteronomy 28:13, which says, "*If you listen to these commands of the Lord your God that I am giving you today, and if you carefully obey them, the Lord will make you the Head, and not the tail, and you will always be on top and never at the bottom.*" I want my kids to always remember to be leaders, they should lead their friends into good things and lead their friends away from bad things.

I pray your girls will have the courage to stand up for what is right!

Polka Dot Plus

Kindergarten and 1st Grade Take Home Activity Sheets

Deuteronomy 28:13 NLT talks about being a leader. It says, "*If you listen to these commands of the Lord your God that I am giving you today, and if you carefully obey them, the Lord will make you the HEAD and NOT the TAIL, and you will always be on top and never at the bottom.*"

Color the puppy below and remember that it's his head that decides where he wants to go and what he wants to do. The head is the leader of the dog. His tail just follows behind.

Read the verses below and fill in the blanks below with the word **RIGHT**.

Do what is _____. Then you will be accepted. If you don't do what is right, sin is waiting at your door to grab you. It longs to have you. But you must rule over it. – Genesis 4:7 NIRV

But even if you suffer for doing what is _____, God will reward you for it. So don't worry or be afraid of their threats. –1 Peter 3:14 NLT

He did what was pleasing in the Lord's sight and followed the example of his ancestor David. He did not turn away from doing what was _____. – 2 Kings 22:2 NLT

All Scripture is inspired by God and is useful to teach us what is true and to make us realize what is wrong in our lives. It corrects us when we are wrong and teaches us to do what is _____. – 2 Timothy 3:16 NLT

2nd and 3rd Grade
Take Home Activity Sheets

The Bible is so **amazing**. It can give us wisdom and insight in **so** many areas of our lives. God will show you the right way to live your life through the words He wrote to you.

Unscramble the words below, place them in the correct part of the scripture verse and discover what God has to say about leadership!

Step 1 – Unscramble the words

dhae   ____ ____ ____ ____

ltia   ____ ____ ____ ____

mmcadsno   ____ ____ ____ ____ ____ ____ ____ ____

dLro   ____ ____ ____ ____

wflloo   ____ ____ ____ ____ ____ ____

tbtomo   ____ ____ ____ ____ ____

Step 2 - Fill in the blanks of the scripture verse below with the correct unscrambled word from step one.

The **LORD** will make you the ____ ____ ____ ____,

not the ____ ____ ____ ____.

If you pay attention to the ____ ____ ____ ____ ____ ____ ____ ____

of the ____ ____ ____ ____ your God that I give you this day and carefully

____ ____ ____ ____ ____ ____ them, you will always be at the top, never

at the ____ ____ ____ ____ ____ ____.

Step 3 – Check your answer by reading Deuteronomy 28:13 NIV.

WORD LIST

lord *tail* *bottom* *commands* *follow* *head*

4th and 5th Grade
Take Home Activity Sheets

The Bible is so **amazing**. It can give us wisdom and insight in **so** many areas of our lives. It can help us know how to be a kind friend, a good daughter, a hard worker, and many, many other things. God is there to help you make the right choices and live a life that honors Him.

Step 1 - Read each verse below and fill in the blank. All scripture NIV

"But even if you should _____ for what is right, you are blessed.

Do not fear what they fear; do not be frightened." – 1 Peter 3:14

"Fear of man will prove to be a snare, but whoever _____ in the

LORD is kept safe." –Proverbs 29:25

"If you do what is right, will you not be _____? But if you do

not do what is right, sin is crouching at your door; it desires to have you, but you must

master it." – Genesis 4:7

"Am I now trying to win the approval of men, or of God? Or am I trying to please

men? If I were still trying to please men, I would _____ be a

servant of Christ." – Galations 1:10

233

"He did what was right in the eyes of the LORD and walked in all the ways of his

father _____, not turning aside to the right or to the left."

– 2 Kings 22:2

"All Scripture is God-breathed and is _____ for teaching, rebuk-

ing, correcting and training in righteousness." – 2 Timothy 3:16

"…for they loved _____ from men more than praise from God."

– John 12:43

Step 2 – Circle the first letter of each missing word from the previous page, and put that letter into the blank spaces below to find out what God wants you to do!

God wants you to ____ ____ ____ ____ ____   ____ ____!

Word List

David	*praise*	*useful*	*accepted*
suffer	*trusts*	*not*	

Polka Dot Party

Poka Dot Party is a night for your girls to connect, invite their friends, and have FUN! Put together an exciting, special event for the girls to simply enjoy each other, do some fun activities, and tell their friends how FUN Polka Dot Girls is!

This is a great way to give the girls something exciting to look forward to and when they're excited about something – they tell their friends! Really encourage them to bring a friend from school or their neighborhood with them.

There is no "lesson" for this night, because we simply want the girls to connect. I promise you, if their friends have an amazing night – they will want to come back! This is a great way to introduce the girls in your community to your church and leaders. Make sure your event is AWESOME!

At the end of the evening, be sure to send invited friends a promotional piece about your ministry. This is a great way to invite them back for the weekend with their parents!

Polka Dot Party

Theme: Movie Night

Food: Popcorn and Candy of course!

Activity: Pick a fun movie that focuses on friendship. Make sure that you pick age appropriate, G rated material.

Set up: If you have access to a large screen, this is the best way to watch a movie! If not, use a large TV and clear out space for the girls to gather in front of it on the floor!

For Fun: Encourage the girls to bring blankets and pillows and let them lounge around while they watch their movie.

Polka Dot Party
MOVIE NIGHT

Polka Dot Party
MOVIE NIGHT

POLKA DOT GIRLS MOVIE NIGHT!

Come for a fun night to hang out with the girls and do crafts, games, and have snacks! Bring a friend!!

Where _____

When _____

POLKA DOT GIRLS MOVIE NIGHT!

Come for a fun night to hang out with the girls and do crafts, games, and have snacks! Bring a friend!!

Where _____

When _____